DENALI'S
West Buttress

DENALI'S
West Buttress

A CLIMBER'S GUIDE
TO MOUNT McKINLEY'S
CLASSIC ROUTE

Colby Coombs

A BRIEF HISTORY OF THE WEST BUTTRESS
ROUTE'S ORIGINS & PHOTOGRAPHS

Bradford Washburn

THE
MOUNTAINEERS

Published by
The Mountaineers
1001 SW Klickitat Way, Suite 201
Seattle, WA 98134

Published simultaneously in Great Britain by Cordee, 3a DeMontfort Street, Leicester, England, LE1 7HD

Manufactured in Canada

Edited by Deborah Kaufmann
Maps by Caitlin Palmer
Cover design by Patrick Lanfear and Helen Cherullo
Book design by Alice C. Merrill
Book layout by Ani Rucki

Cover photograph: View of Denali's West Buttress. ©Bradford Washburn

Library of Congress Cataloging-in-Publication Data
Coombs, Colby.
　　　Denali's West Buttress: a climber's guide to Mount McKinley's classic route / Colby Coombs : introduction & photographs, Bradford Washburn.
　　　　　p.　　cm.
　　　ISBN 0-89886-516-6
　　　　1. Mountaineering—Alaska—McKinley, Mount—Guidebooks.
　　2. McKinley, Mount (Alaska)—Guidebooks. I. Title.
　　GV199.42.A42M3223　1997　　　　　　　　　97-30735
　　796.52'2'097983—dc21　　　　　　　　　　　CIP

Table of Contents

Approach, Route, Descent

Washburn Photographs

Foreword

SINCE THE HUDSON STUCK PARTY FIRST CLIMBED the south summit in 1913, some 19,250 climbers have attempted to reach Denali's summit. During the 1997 mountaineering season, this figure will most likely reach twenty thousand—or more. As a rule, in an average year only 50 percent of the expected twelve hundred climbers succeed in reaching the summit, while one hundred climbers succumb to either altitude sickness or frostbite, and twelve major rescues are necessary.

Over the past forty years, the vast majority of Denali's climbers— approximately 80 percent of all the climbers in any given year—have used the West Buttress as their primary route to the mountain's summit. To date, this beautiful but moderate route has seen more than four hundred accidents involving crevasse plunges, climbing falls, brutal weather, and/or altitude sickness. Thirty-four people have died attempting this route.

The National Park Service expects the number of climbers to increase each year because Denali's summit is the highest in North America. The ranger camp on the West Buttress, at 14,200 feet, serves as headquarters for the National Park Service patrols and is normally staffed with five volunteers, including a climbing doctor and one mountaineering ranger. Each season, this acclimated and highly trained mountaineering patrol deals with numerous problems ranging from issues of sanitation to dangerous rescues to illegal guiding, and more.

Since the West Buttress route was first climbed by Dr. Washburn's expedition in 1951, there have been many extreme episodes of near-miss survivals—as well as tragic deaths. Today, some climbers regularly use the "West Butt" to prepare themselves for harder routes. The route has gained a reputation for being technically easy; subsequently, its severity is underestimated. The West Buttress's subjective Alaskan grade II difficulty rating has caused more than one

(#8277) View of the Alaska Range from the southwest with the Kitchatna Spires in the foreground. ©Bradford Washburn

9

Mt. Foraker

Mt. Crosson

Denali

South   North

Mt. Dickey

Moose's Tooth

Ruth
Gorge

#8693

expedition to abandon self-sufficiency. Surprised and unprepared climbers frequently call for a rescue after discovering the mountain's rage. Numerous articles have been written about climbers dying on Denali, and in some the writers state that at least the deceased were doing what they loved when they died. I have never heard of, nor personally rescued, anyone on Denali who wanted to be left behind while claiming, "Leave me here so I can die doing what I love to do!" Success in mountaineering should not be measured solely by whether or not you reach the summit, but also by achieving the satisfaction of carrying out a safe and well-planned trip on one of the most extreme mountains on earth.

Every year hundreds of people attempt the West Buttress route expecting a wilderness experience. As well, they become part of a large international community sharing the common goal of reaching Denali's summit. During the peak months of May and June, in excess of two hundred people are likely to be found camping at the 14,200-foot Basin Camp. The presence of such large numbers has led to safety concerns ranging from sanitation to overloading the fixed lines on the Headwall. Hopefully these problems will be successfully addressed without necessitating further regulations.

Many resources concerning Denali are already available. Colby Coombs's *Denali's West Buttress: A Climber's Guide to Mount McKinley's Classic Route* is an excellent addition to this list, providing the West Buttress climber with a guidebook suitable for carrying on the mountain. Safe climbing to you all.

Daryl R. Miller, High Altitude Mountaineering Ranger

(#8693) View of Denali from the southeast with the Ruth Gorge in the foreground. ©Bradford Washburn

#7976

North Summit

South Summit

△ 14,200'

Mt. Huntington

Mt. Hunter

Kahiltna Pass

Kahiltna Dome

Mt. Crosson

Preface

AFTER YEARS OF CLIMBING DENALI'S WEST BUTTRESS and sharing the mountain's beauty and severity with climbers from around the world, I realized there was a growing need for a guidebook to this route. The exact moment of convincing must have been when, while standing on the southeast fork of the Kahiltna Glacier, a foreign climber asked me, "Which way is Denali?"

Given the enormity of the surroundings, I knew how easily a climber could feel swallowed up and disoriented, despite the wealth of McKinley guidebooks already in print. Only upon researching, however, did I learn with surprise that not one of these books was devoted specifically to the West Buttress, nor was any suitable for bringing along on the climb. Already in the habit of carrying a Washburn print of the route to show climbers, it struck me that arranging a collection of his photographs in guidebook format would appeal to those desiring route information. The name *Washburn* is synonymous with the West Buttress, so well does this pioneering mountaineer know the terrain. His photographs are so detailed and revealing that they transcend any language barrier or lack of proficiency in reading topographical maps.

In an effort to complement Washburn's photos, I have gathered thoughts and ideas about how to safely and successfully climb the West Buttress from climbers who, collectively, have made a total of over one hundred ascents. Having climbed the mountain a dozen times myself and having carefully observed other guides who have climbed it three times more than I, I know there are camping and traveling strategies unique to McKinley and, specifically, to the West Buttress. Making this information available can only help to decrease the number and severity of accidents and environmental problems. Along with all the pertinent route information, this guide also includes a crash course on Denali's climbing history, its geology, health concerns specific to climbing, and, even more specifically, to women climbers.

(#7976) Denali from the west. ©Bradford Washburn

Denali's West Buttress is intended to be a resource for experienced mountaineers and winter campers. The book does not provide either the experience or judgment necessary to safely climb Denali—each individual climber must bring his or her own resources and capabilities to the climb. Conditions are constantly changing and photographs cannot be relied upon to accurately represent them. The measurements given for the marked route, camps, and distances are all approximate. There is no trail.

The word *Denali,* which means "the High One," is a Native Alaskan name for Mount McKinley. The names *Denali* and *Mount McKinley* are used interchangeably throughout the text.

All who have contributed to this guidebook know that whoever climbs the West Buttress will come away with a greater appreciation of the extremes in which beauty is revealed. It is our hope that *Denali's West Buttress: A Climber's Guide to Mount McKinley's Classic Route* will augment every step of your journey.

Colby Coombs

(#7474) Talkeetna in 1970 with the Chulitna, Susitna, and Talkeetna Rivers in the foreground. Denali (top center) is 60 miles from Talkeetna. ©Bradford Washburn

Acknowledgments

Denali's West Buttress: A Climber's Guide to Mount McKinley's Classic Route represents a true collaborative effort. I could not have written this guidebook without the assistance of the following individuals, who contributed greatly to both the editing and content of the work.

Phil Brease, a noted National Park Service geologist, works for the Resource Management Division of Denali National Park and Preserve. For the past seven years, Brease has been conducting research studies concerning the glaciology and geology of Mount McKinley. He has supervised field studies on several of the surrounding glaciers in Denali National Park, tracking their movements and surges.

Ted Fathauer is the "Meteorologist in Charge" at the National Weather Service Forecast Office in Fairbanks, Alaska. Fathauer has studied Denali's violent weather patterns for over twenty years and has predicted some of the major storms in the mountain's recent weather history.

Dr. Colin Grissom, a pulmonary specialist and accomplished climber, has spent years carrying out medical research on Denali. He has written and published numerous articles pertaining to high altitude illnesses and has volunteered the past six years as physician on National Park Service patrols. In addition to the West Buttress, Colin has climbed the West Rib and Cassin routes.

Daryl R. Miller has been a high altitude mountaineering ranger in Denali National Park and Preserve since 1991. Miller has spent over two hundred days at 14,200 feet or higher on the West Buttress, participating in National Park Service mountaineering patrols. His role in numerous lifesaving high altitude helicopter rescues has earned him the United States' Valor Award and Italy's International Alpine Solidarity Award. In 1995, Miller completed the first winter circumnavigation of the Denali-Foraker Massif—a 350-mile/560-kilometer, forty-five-day "outing" with fellow Talkeetnan Mark Stasik.

Brian Okonek has spent the past twenty-four years climbing, guiding, and photographing the mountains of Alaska. As director of Alaska-Denali Guiding, Inc., in Talkeetna, he has led more than thirty expeditions on Denali and fifty throughout the Alaska Range. An avid explorer and naturalist, Okonek has numerous first ascents to his credit and is fascinated by the wildlife of Denali National Park and Preserve.

Caitlin Palmer, an artist, climber, and Denali guide, codirects the Alaska Mountaineering School in Talkeetna. She participated in the 1994 Women's Breast Cancer Expedition and led the 1997 Cancer Survivors Expedition on the West Buttress.

Dr. Bradford Washburn, one of the world's leading experts on Mount McKinley, provides a rich historical account from his pioneering first ascent of the West Buttress route in 1951. Brad has devoted a large part of his life to exploring, mapping, and photographing Mount McKinley and the Alaska Range. His photographs provide the standard of excellence for climbers seeking route information.

Thanks to Talkeetna historian **Roberta Sheldon** for writing the section on Talkeetna. Many thanks also go to **Diane Okonek**, **Roger Robinson**, and **Blaine Smith** for their valuable contributions to this guide.

Colby Coombs

A Brief History of the
West Buttress Route's Origins
by Bradford Washburn

THE FIRST SIX ASCENTS OF 20,320-FOOT Mount McKinley were all made by almost exactly the same route: Wonder Lake, Cache Creek, McGonagall Pass, Muldrow Glacier, Karstens Ridge, and Harper Glacier. This was the route of the pioneers. For almost half a century the legend had persisted that this great peak was virtually unclimbable from any direction but the northeast.

Once McKinley had been successfully climbed by the four-man team of Hudson Stuck, Harry Karstens, Walter Harper, and Robert Tatum on June 7, 1913, nobody gave any serious thought to the possibility of another way to the top until our National Geographic flights around and over it in July 1936. During these flights and after studying the photographs they yielded, a technically easy approach from the west side immediately became apparent. However, the seemingly endless hike from civilization to the beginning of the real climbing on the upper reaches of the Kahiltna Glacier looked far too long and impractical when compared with the time-honored 35-mile trek from Wonder Lake by way of Muldrow Glacier. Then, after completion of a good road from park headquarters to Wonder Lake at the end of World War II, nobody gave any thought to a possible alternative. However, during the course of the huge U.S. Army Alaskan Test Expedition in July 1942, Einar Nilsson and I were collecting parachuted supplies way up in 18,000-foot Denali Pass and—seizing our first chance for a really good view of magnificient Mount Foraker—happpened to look down the west side of the mountain. As we spotted the Kahiltna Galcier 10,000 feet below us, we suddenly realized that almost all of that side of McKinley was nothing but a safe, steep, chilly scramble.

Toward the end of the war, my interest in the McKinley area steadily grew when I was a member of the team that investigated the terrible crash of an Army C-47 into Mount Deception in the fall of 1944 and took part in the winter test of U.S. Air Force emergency equipment in the Silverthrone area in 1945. These experiences led me to write a ten-page article in the 1947 *American Alpine Journal (AAJ)* entitled, "Mount McKinley from the North and West," which came to the attention of readers while my wife Barbara and I were high on the great peak in April, May, and June of that year. We were members of a large expedition which began the survey that later resulted in today's Mount McKinley Map. We also carried out a major cosmic ray study program for the University of Chicago's Department of Physics and, of all things, the U.S. Office of Naval Research (ONR). Two of the illustrations in that *AAJ* article (plates 7 and 8) focused on McKinley's West Buttress as a new, easy direct route to the top, and caused Jim Gale and me to look down the west side of Denali Pass with even more intense interest than Einar Nilsson and I had done four years before.

A brief trip with Jim Gale to the McKinley area on behalf of ONR late in the summer of 1949 convinced me of two things: firstly, that the West Buttress was clearly the shortest, easiest, and safest way to climb Mount McKinley, and secondly, that the lengthy approach to the beginning of the real climb could be virtually eliminated by easy ski plane landings almost anywhere on the upper reaches of the Kahiltna Glacier.

Another event occurred in 1949 that would make this sort of ski plane landing both easy and economical: my lifelong friend Dr. Terris Moore became the second president of the University of Alaska and brought with him one of the first Super Cub 125 airplanes with hydraulically operated ski wheels ever to fly in Alaska. With such a plane it would be easy to take off on wheels from any normal landing field and land with safety and ease on any reasonably smooth, snow-covered glacier. As a pilot myself, I was postive that one could easily land almost anywhere on Kahiltna Galcier between 7,000 and 10,000 feet—even as high as 14,000 feet if an emergency situation required it.

With this intriguing background, in the winter of 1951, I heard through the mountaineering grapevine that a Denver expedition, tempted by my 1947 *AAJ* article, was planning to attempt an ascent of Mount McKinley's West Buttress during the coming spring or summer. The temptation was too great to resist. Who were they?

Was there any possibility that I might be able to join them? The leader was Dr. Henry Buchtel of Denver, and I called him on the telephone. His reply was instant, enthusiastic, and "yes!" Two more speedy telephone calls added Jim Gale and Bill Hackett, two of my 1947 McKinley partners who had looked down on the upper part of the West Buttress with almost as much original interest as I had. The Denver team was going to do the first geologic research on the west side of McKinley—why couldn't we ask the ONR to arrange some air support for our little expedition which, after all, was going to determine whether this new route would be also the answer to their search for a shorter, easier route to Denali Pass. Before a week had passed, we had put together a large, enthusiastic team which not only might make the first ascent of McKinley's West Buttress, but do good geologic work, complete the mapping of the west side of our big adversary, and also clear up any questions related to how difficult this ascent might be. In a few more days, the ONR gave us a promise of total air support for our party from our old friends in the Tenth Rescue Squadron, Alaskan Air Command.

The original Denver plan was to approach the West Buttress from the north, moving by pack train from Wonder Lake to Straightaway Glacier, and thence to 10,000-foot Kahiltna Pass by way of the upper basin of Peters Glacier. Our new battleplan was now to have the rest of us climb simultaneously to a base camp at Kahiltna Pass from the Kahiltna side.

Mel Griffiths, Barry Bishop, John Ambler, and Jerry More left Wonder Lake with expert horse packer Carl Anderson on June 23, 1951. On June 18 and 19, Terry Moore flew Henry Buchtel, Jim Gale, Bill Hackett, and me to an excellent 7,650-foot landing spot on the Kahiltna Glacier, after taking off from from the nearby landing strip at the end of Chelatna Lake . Even Terry's wife, Katrina, came in on one of the flights and brought us a delicious fresh lake trout for supper. The ONR's promise of air support was fulfilled on June 22 when a Tenth Rescue C-47 parachuted and free-fall dropped almost all of our gear at Kahiltna Pass—with scarcely a single damaged item! Three days later, Terry Moore landed there at 10,000 feet right beside our tents, proving that all sorts of relatively high air support would be easy for a future ONR expedition if it was needed.

On June 30, the geologic arm of our team safely joined us at

Dr. Henry Buchtel   Bill Hackett
Dr. Terris Moore   Dr. Bradford Washburn   Jim Gale   #57-5732

*(#57-5732) Members of the first ascent team and their pilot,
Terris Moore, land on the Kahiltna Glacier, June 1951.
©Bradford Washburn*

Base Camp, having taken only a week to get there, all the way from
Wonder Lake—even having detoured enough on the way to make
the first ascent of Peters Dome, in order to put a survey target on its
summit for us. Weeks later we saw the target clearly all the way from
Wonder Lake.

We all climbed McKinley early in July along exactly the route
described in that 1947 AAT proposal—and also climbed Kahiltna
Dome in order to make important survey observations there. The
view from its 12,525-foot summit is one of the most magnificent
mountain panoramas in the world, with Mounts McKinley, Hunter,
and Foraker flanking the huge Kahiltna Glacier. We rode out a ter-
rific thunderstorm there one afternoon, cozily sheltered in a big
igloo that we'd built for exactly that purpose.

When that 1951 expedition drew to a close, it not only had solved
one of McKinley's most important climbing secrets, but had also
yielded a remarkable geologic collection and given the ONR the
information it needed in order to plan its high-altitude laboratory at
Denali Pass. But the lab never developed beyond the dream stage
as, by the mid-fifties, the great accelerators in the lowlands were

producing collisions between tiny particles of matter which were far more dramatic at sea level than those which cosmic radiation had recorded at Denali Pass fifty years earlier.

Great changes have taken place in the Alaska Range during this last half-century. Our 1947 party had lived on McKinley from March to June and had developed a deep respect for it—not only because of the beauty of our surroundings but also because of its often long, vicious, and violent storms. And, on our way down Karstens Ridge, we had the amazing experience of being the first party ever to meet another group of climbers as they were toiling upward toward Browne Tower. Barbara and I were the first two people ever to meet anyone else on Mount McKinley!

On June 3, 1997, as incredible as it may seem, the ten-thousandth climber (Bruce MacDonald of Nashua, New Hampshire) reached the summit of Denali, which has now regained its old and revered Native Alaskan name. My generation was lucky to have the privilege of knowing, in person, many of the real pioneers—men like Charley McGonagall, Billy Taylor, Harry Karstens, Belmore Browne, and Don Sheldon—and to work our way up many of the ridges on which no one had ever set foot before.

Denali, by even its easiest route, will never be "an easy day for a lady"! If you're reasonably experienced on high, frigid ice and rock, a good cold-weather camper, and favored by the weather gods, the West Buttress may turn out to be a fine, brief, and rewarding experience—a sort of tiny polar expedition in three dimensions. You'll also learn that what you once *did* up there won't yield half as many vivid memories as those about the wonderful companions with whom you lived and struggled and climbed.

But if you run into really bad weather above 17,000 feet, you should remember the story told by Doug Scott and Dougal Haston, in 1976, clearly the two most competent and experienced climbers in the world, as they approached the summit of McKinley in one of its often harsh moments. "We had climbed roped, simultaneously, front-pointing forever into a revived storm and relentless wind. *Everything was cold, even our souls.* Frostbite was waiting to jump at

(#57-5851) Hackett and Gale pack survey equipment on the first ascent of Kahiltna Dome, West Buttress in the background, June 26, 1951. ©Bradford Washburn

Upper Kahiltna Glacier

#57-5851

Mt. Foraker

Mt. Crosson

#57-5893

the slightest weakness, but both of us played our own winning game with it. McKinley's climate is tough. We were drawing heavily on all our Himalayan experience just to survive, and it was a respectful pair that finally stood on the summit ridge."

Don't let the West Buttress route fool you, despite the fact that it is, indeed, the easiest, shortest, safest way to the top of McKinley. If you're lucky, you'll take about three weeks to make the round trip. Some climbers, with a combination of favorable weather, good luck, and experience, will make it faster than that. But don't rush, remember that just one more light relay of food and fuel into your 17,000-foot final camp will easily get you through that unexpected last storm. It's far better to end your climb that way than it is to have to give up and retreat only a day or two before that hurricane blows itself out and good weather returns or to make a try for the summit in weather during which you should have stayed in camp. In fact, your chances of success of the West Buttress are virtually certain if you plan for a month on the mountain instead of just three weeks.

I hope you're as lucky as we were in 1951 and only have to wait out a couple of stormy days in two igloos at Windy Corner—which we named for good reason. But don't forget that, in late May of 1947, our two teams, at Browne Tower and Denali Pass, were completely pinned down for nine days in one of McKinley's violent reactions to having people on its slopes.

Success on Mount McKinley is infinitely rewarding—by any route. In 1913, the first-ascent team reached the summit on a magnificent, calm, almost cloudless day. Years later, Robert Tatum described his experience more briefly and impressively than anyone else: "The view from the top of Mount McKinley is like looking out the windows of Heaven!"

page 24: *(#57-5893) Hackett and Gale ascending fixed lines on the Headwall. ©Bradford Washburn*
page 25: *(#57-5929) Hackett and Gale on the summit, 5:30 PM, July 10, 1951. ©Bradford Washburn*

Before
•
You
•
Go
•

A History of Denali National Park and Preserve

*W*hen the lengthy approaches and intricate glacier systems around Denali were first explored, and its summits finally climbed for the first time, neither the great mountain nor its surrounding country were part of a national park. Imagine how remote Alaska was in 1917 when a 9,468-square-mile area of boreal forest, tundra, and mountains was designated Mount McKinley National Park, the first park under the newly established National Park Service (NPS). The name would eventually be changed in 1980 to Denali National Park and Preserve (DNP&P).

The famous naturalist Charles Sheldon was instrumental in the park's conception. From 1906 to 1908, he observed wildlife and collected specimens in the foothills north of McKinley for natural history museums. The energetic and curious Sheldon scrambled to the base of Denali's 14,000-foot/4,300-meter north face (Wickersham Wall) and watched avalanches crash onto the glacier. He was impressed by this habitat which could support an abundance of moose, caribou, Dall sheep, and grizzly bear, and was concerned about the area's uncontrolled "market hunting." Hunters were shooting wild game in large numbers to feed nearby gold prospectors, railroad workers, and the growing population of Fairbanks. The spectacular sight of Mount McKinley—possibly the highest uplift above snow line of any mountain in the world—and the many other mountains of the Alaska Range further impressed him. It became his life mission to preserve the region's natural habitat so that future generations might experience the area as he had.

Harry Karstens, a great friend of Sheldon and a member of Hudson Stuck's team during the first ascent of Denali's south peak, was appointed first superintendent of McKinley National Park in 1921. It was a position in which few friends were made. Besides the laborious duty of building a headquarters and patrol cabins, Karstens had to enforce NPS regulations upon free-spirited Alaskans. First and foremost on his list of things to do was to stop the market hunters.

In a continued effort to protect wildlife by protecting the greater ecosystem, the original park has been expanded several times to its present six million square acres. Over the years, better access and promotion of the park have greatly increased visitation. The NPS's mandate for preserving wilderness while making it available to the public—"multiple use"—creates a tug-of-war and greater challenge every year. Many regulations have been drawn up in an attempt to protect and preserve the area. Denali and the glaciers north of the summit are designated wilderness areas and airplane landings are prohibited. Expeditions from the north have to endure overland approaches starting at low elevations and to this day enjoy pioneer-like ascents of Denali. On the south side, bush pilots have been flying climbers to 7,200 feet/2,200 meters onto the Kahiltna Glacier ever since Washburn's first ascent in 1951. The current landing site is on the Kahiltna Glacier, 5 miles/8 kilometers south of where Washburn's team landed in order to be outside the wilderness boundary. In 1980, Denali Park was again expanded to include the glaciers and peaks to roughly tree line on the south side of the mountain. This addition is not designated wilderness and planes are allowed to land within its boundaries.

Brian Okonek

A History of Denali's National Park Service

*T*he early superintendents of Mount McKinley National Park knew firsthand the seriousness of the mountain and the difficulty of rescues from its slopes. In an effort to minimize accidents, regulations were passed requiring all climbing expeditions to be first approved by the NPS. Rangers corresponded with expeditions and checked equipment to satisfy these requirements. In 1948, to better facilitate any rescues that might occur in the park, rangers were sent to the first NPS mountain climbing and rescue training school.

Until the mid-1950s, all expeditions checked in at McKinley National Park headquarters, located at McKinley Park Village, on their way to the north side of the mountain (see map, page 31). When the Muldrow Glacier surged in 1957, making it impossible to climb the standard northern route, air access to the West Buttress began in earnest. By the late 1950s, Talkeetna became the major jumping-off point for climbers destined for Denali. Required NPS equipment checks at park headquarters, 125 miles/201 kilometers north of Talkeetna, were too far out of the way. Don Sheldon, a local glacier pilot, became the first Talkeetna-based National Park representative when he was authorized in 1958 to conduct the required equipment checks.

For the next decade, the park superintendents tried to impress upon climbers the need to be adequately prepared for the mountain. One inquiry into climbing the mountain in 1965 was answered by Acting Superintendent Arthur Hayes: "Don't sell Denali short; the regular routes may be technically easy, but the subarctic conditions of the area are such that even mountaineers of vast Himalayan experience, such as the late Lionel Terray, are astonished by their severity." The NPS's attempt to safeguard climbers resulted in a long and cumbersome list of requirements. Over the years, this list has been overhauled and simplified, and continues to evolve in the NPS's attempt to manage climbing.

The first climbing ranger position was established in 1973 when twenty-two expedition teams attempted Denali. Three years later, the first climbing ranger patrol was organized to make a traverse of the mountain and be available in a support role in case of an accident. In 1977, two rangers were stationed seasonally in Talkeetna, and in 1984 a year-round district ranger took up residence in order to effectively manage mountaineering and other issues facing the south side of DNP&P. In 1997, a ranger station was built in Talkeetna to handle the annual increase in numbers of climbers. Continued NPS presence in Talkeetna has established a division in the park in terms of management: the north side deals primarily with wildlife visitors and the south side with climbers.

Currently, the NPS conducts multiple, twenty-four-hour-a-day, overlapping ranger patrols on the West Buttress over the course of the climbing season. Patrols are essentially climbing expeditions led by climbing rangers who choose five to eight experienced volunteers to accompany them. These patrols monitor environmental practices and park regulations, and assist with emergencies. Despite rumors to

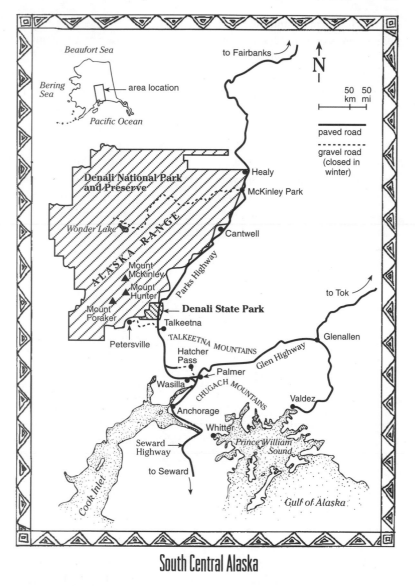

Beaufort Sea

Bering Sea

area location

Pacific Ocean

to Fairbanks

N

50   50
km   mi

paved road

gravel road
(closed in
winter)

Denali National Park and Preserve

Healy

McKinley Park

Wonder Lake

ALASKA RANGE

Cantwell

Mount McKinley

Mount Hunter

Parks Highway

to Tok

Mount Foraker

Denali State Park

Talkeetna

Petersville

TALKEETNA MOUNTAINS

Hatcher Pass

Glenallen

Glen Highway

Palmer

Wasilla

CHUGACH MOUNTAINS

Valdez

Anchorage

Whittier

Prince William Sound

Seward Highway

to Seward

Cook Inlet

Gulf of Alaska

South Central Alaska

the contrary, they are *not* on the mountain to mark crevasses, put in fixed lines, pack garbage out, or be a collection depot for extra fuel.

From 1982 to 1989, Dr. Peter Hackett directed a high-altitude research station at the 14,200-foot/4,300-meter basin on the West Buttress. In the search for information concerning altitude-related illnesses, Hackett and his team of doctors and nurses conducted experiments on climbers and military personnel arranged to be flown up from sea level. By virtue of its location high on the mountain, the research station was able to assist climbers suffering from all ailments and injuries, including those that were related to altitude. In 1990, the NPS took over where Hackett's team left off by maintaining a smaller station at the same location. Presently, the camp's primary function is for ranger patrols to maintain reliable communications and provisions to care for sick or injured climbers, and it is supplied by both military and NPS helicopters.

In 1995, the NPS established a second ranger patrol camp at the Kahiltna Base Landing Strip (7,200 feet/2,200 meters on the southeast fork of the Kahiltna Glacier). NPS rangers help keep the mountain clean by ensuring that all expeditions properly deal with their garbage and human waste and by levying hefty fines against violators.

Brian Okonek

A History of Guiding

*A*long with Mount Rainier and the Grand Teton, Mount McKinley is a center for mountain guiding in the United States. In 1940, the NPS received its first request, from an Italian named Piero Ghiglione, for a guide to lead an ascent of Mount McKinley. The superintendent could not find anyone who was enthusiastic over the prospect or qualified to accept the responsibility of guiding, nor would he authorize any of the park personnel to officially participate in the climb. The superintendent's personal opinion was that Ghiglione was expecting a great deal to have a party and climbing companion do everything through no particular effort by him. The expedition never did materialize, possibly because of World War II.

Throughout the 1940s and 1950s there were no mountaineering guides available who specialized in climbing Denali. The need and incentive for a guiding business on the High One had not yet been established. The year 1960 marked the first guided expedition and the twenty-first ascent of Denali's south summit. But the profession got off to a rocky start. While the group was descending from Denali Pass, a climbing fall necessitated one of the largest rescue efforts in the mountain's history.

In 1963, the first special-use permit authorizing guided expeditions up Mount McKinley was issued. At the time, Superintendent Samuel King envisioned a guided expedition as "a group composed of people who have similar interests but do not have a party of their own or lack the experience to do the climb on their own. This does not mean that novices will be allowed to attempt the climb. Each applicant must show that he has a reasonable amount of climbing experience."

The expedition did not reach the summit. According to Bradford Washburn, who kept meticulous records of every Mount McKinley climb up to and including number one hundred, one member of the expedition suffered frostbite and there were reports of "confusion and dissension in the party." Don Sheldon, one of the pioneering glacier pilots, was left unpaid for flying the group of ten people and two thousand pounds of gear to the mountain. The expedition was not a model to follow and the permit was dropped. Guiding on North America's highest mountain had been short-lived.

No guiding service existed until 1969 when Alaska Mountain Guides became the first company to specialize in guiding on Denali. The company name was changed to Genet Expeditions by its founder, director, and chief guide, Ray Genet. The age of guiding now had begun on the mountain. Genet's "to the summit" style was controversial, but the NPS accepted the fact that his services were indeed needed.

As the number of prospective Denali "clients" increased, the NPS decided to authorize additional special-use permits to qualified applicants. Before long, a variety of companies were offering guided expeditions and their presence on the mountain became commonplace. The NPS's concerns over the safety and business practices of the guiding companies initiated a change in how companies were authorized to guide on Mount McKinley. A concession permit system was established in 1980, providing the NPS with regulatory authority over guiding companies. Six companies were given authority to lead expeditions on Denali and other mountains within the wilderness boundary of the park. In 1996, when 1,148 climbers attempted Denali, at least 20 percent were members of guided expeditions. Guiding on Denali has established an undisputed track record for safety and a high summit success rate.

Brian Okonek

Guiding Companies at Denali National Park and Preserve

*S*ix companies are currently authorized by Denali National Park and Preserve to guide on Denali (see Appendix C). Each company is closely monitored by the NPS for client safety, business practices, and environmental issues. These services offer a variety of guiding styles and climbing routes to the public. Any guiding company that you consider climbing with must be authorized by DNP&P. Illegally guided trips have been turned back in Talkeetna and the guides fined and even arrested.

A person joining a guided expedition will benefit by having the logistical preparations for the climb completed for them, the consultation of experts concerning equipment and training, and supervision and instruction on the mountain to insure safety. Joining a group of climbers with similar goals and having the guide's knowledge and experience behind each decision provides many people with the best possible chance of having a successful experience on Denali.

Denali is a tremendous mountaineering challenge by any route. Even a member of a guided expedition requires previous mountaineering experience. Guiding companies screen prospective clients for backpacking, winter camping, and mountaineering experience, as well as general fitness. The magnitude of Denali requires that each team member be a strong participant in the climb.

Mountaineering has its inherent risks. While joining a guided expedition might reduce the dangers of climbing Denali, it cannot eliminate them. Clients must acknowledge that they understand the risks associated with mountaineering and accept the responsibility of participating in a climbing expedition.

Brian Okonek

The Geology of Denali National Park and Preserve

*D*escribing geology, or telling the geologic story of any area, can be an intimidating task, even for the seasoned geologist. First, the story is one of history, and not of a few hundred or thousand years, but millions, hundreds of millions, and even billions of years. Second, the story is almost always about large hunks of real estate. Denali National Park and Preserve totals six million acres, an area roughly the size of Massachusetts. Third, the story is never about small, simple backwater environments, but rather of deep and shallow oceans, midocean rifts and volcanic island arcs, uplifted and eroded mountains, rivers and lakes that have come and gone—and, of course, some large and small swampy backwater conditions as well.

Indeed, Denali geology is no piece of cake—or should I say, "layer cake," as places such as the Grand Canyon are often described. In fact, I like to describe the geology of Denali as a mix of several well-known western parks. The recipe entails placing the sediments of the Grand Canyon, the plutonic rocks of Yosemite, and the volcanics of Mount Rainier into a blender. Turn the blender on briefly to CHOP, layer the mixture as a parfait, and serve with large quantities of ice from the likes of Glacier Bay National Park.

Alaskan geology in general, and that of Denali Park specifically, is poorly understood. The present level of understanding is about where it was for the Lower 48, thirty to fifty years ago. Consequently, the story has many gaps and requires significant leaps of faith, but does not lack in interest or intrigue.

Denali probably began in a relatively quiet near-shore ocean environment about one billion or more years ago, as a northern tip to ancestral North America. Sands, shales, and limestones with occasional volcanic flows and intrusions were laid down in these surroundings for a period of about nine hundred million years. These rocks were tectonically altered—metamorphosed—several times after their deposition to become schists, marbles, and greenstones of the Yukon-Tanana terrane, a portion of which makes up the northern part of the park. The alteration of these marine rocks records the beginning of a long history of a north-south tectonic compression of Alaska that has formed the existing Alaska Mountain Range and perhaps several other ancestral Alaska ranges over a period of several hundred million years.

While this earliest mountain building was going on in central Alaska, ocean-shelf to deep-basin conditions were interspersed among these rising landforms, probably somewhat similar to conditions in the Prince William Sound and Cook Inlet region today. This environment created the shales, mudstones, and graywacke of the terrane known as the Nixon Fork. Also included in the Nixon Fork are discontinuous east-west limestone bodies of 360 to 390 million years ago (MYA), coral reef deposits identical to those of the present-day Bahama Islands. Marine fossil evidence in these rocks, and plant fossils found in overlying freshwater sediments (the Mount Dall Conglomerate), suggest a close affinity to Russian Siberia from at least 250 to 390 MYA, when the Laurasian Continents were closer to the equator. Today, these rocks make up some of the higher northeast summits in the park, including Mount Pendleton and Scott Peak, as well as much of the unnamed highlands from Dall Glacier westerly to Shellabarger Pass.

Sometime during the first half of the Mesozoic Period, 150 to 250 MYA, Pacific Plate movement shifted to a more northerly direction, and increased rates of subduction—subsurface sinking of crustal material—and obduction—thrusting of crustal material onto the mainland—became the primary building mechanism of southern Alaska. Smaller slivers of land called microplates, made up of varieties of ocean crustal material, islands, and/or terrestrial sediments, were transported northerly on the larger Pacific Plate, much as a conveyor belt delivers goods from one point to another. Two of these microplates, the McKinley and Pingston terranes, are deep to shallow marine sediments unlike any other nearby marine sediments, and therefore considered by some to be exotic terranes originally deposited somewhere other than where they are now found. These rocks are located in patches in the northern foothills of the range within Denali National Park.

Perhaps an even more exotic sliver, the Chulitna terrane, suggests possible origins from the Southern Pacific, with a transport history that includes a brief stop in the Pacific Northwest before finally arriving at its present position, mostly in Denali National Park (see map, page 31). Fossil occurrences and rock types in the Chulitna terrane—rocks called ophiolites, interbedded basalts, and limestones—suggest a 370 MYA origin, possibly at a Southern Pacific, midocean, spreading rift environment. The ophiolites are followed by the deposition of 220-million-year-old terrestrial red-bed sandstones, of which similar types are found in Southern Idaho. Finally, shallow water marine sediments from local Alaskan sources, 150 to 200 MYA, overlay the ophiolites and red beds. The entire package now sits in the upper Ohio Creek vicinity, along the southeast boundary of the park.

In mid-Cretaceous times, ninety MYA, a large landmass slammed into Alaska, effectively making a new coastline some two hundred kilometers farther south than the previous coastline. The Talkeetna superterrane—a volcanic island arc somewhat like Japan—closed off or collapsed the Susitna Basin along the southern boundary of the ark, and in doing so, compacted shallow marine basin sediments—shales, graywacke, and sandstone—and thrust them up into a new mountain range: the present Alaska Range as we know it. Many of the major peaks immediately east of Mount McKinley—Mounts Mather, Deception, Brooks, and Silverthrone—consist of this Cretaceous rock known as argillite—rhythmic bedded shallow marine sediments. While mountain building and uplift dominated this scene from sixty to ninety MYA in DNP&P, weathering and erosion did its best to keep up, providing a thick accumulation of terrestrial material which has become the Cantwell sediments. These sandstones, shales, and conglomerates were deposited into an east-west trough immediately north of the range, and were slowly folded and faulted from the continuous Pacific Plate migration toward the north.

Molten magma resulting from the superterrane collision intruded the thrusted wedge of argillite to cool and crystallize fifty-six MYA into the granitic rocks of Mounts McKinley, Hunter, Huntington, and many of their supporting buttress ridges. The south peak, or true summit, of Mount McKinley itself is dominantly granitic rock, while the upper approximately 1,500 feet/460 meters of the north peak is a cap of argillite that has provided a jet-black roof over the intruding granite. The magma also intruded the Cantwell Sediments and erupted to the surface as lava flows and ashfalls in the northern foothills, and can be found primarily as basalts and rhyolites in colorful Polychrome Pass and vicinity.

In another burst of magmatic activity about thirty-eight MYA, Mounts Foraker and McGonagall plutons crystallized alongside the existing Mount McKinley granite, and the Mount Galen Volcanics became the surface extrusive counterpart. Some Mount McKinley granite was possibly exhumed at this time, but most of the exposure of the Great One probably consisted of argillite. The Mounts Foraker and McGonagall plutons consist of granodiorite, a granite with very little k-spar, and the Mount Galen volcanics are chiefly tuffs and andesites. These volcanics are speculated to have erupted from a vent on the top of Mount Thoroughfare, which would make the peak the only volcano in DNP&P.

Tectonic forces continued to pressure the Alaskan mainland, forcing the buckling and uplift of the Alaska Range ever higher. Warm climate periods prevailed in the late Tertiary, ten to forty MYA, which rapidly eroded the rising mountains, and small subsiding basins adjacent to the mighty peaks became the collecting centers for the sediment. On the northern side of the range in the Healy area, stream flow was predominantly from the north, which brought sediments up against the wall of the Alaska Range to become the Usibelli Group, the coal-bearing unit that is mined near the town of Healy. This group consists of five formations of stream and lake sediments. These rocks can be found along the park road near the Teklanika and East Fork Toklat Rivers.

While the climate slowly moved from warm, swampy conditions to colder, drier conditions during the last twenty million years, tectonic compression continued to squeeze central Alaska, forcing major fractures in a series of faults known as the Denali fault system. This fault complex stretches over 1,500 miles/2,400 kilometers through Canada and Alaska, and according to some geoscience views, represents the ancestral boundary between the Pacific and North American plates. The McKinley strand of the fault system arcs through the southern third of the park and separates the argillite from the older Nixon Fork terrane in both normal and strike-slip, or right lateral, relationships. The Hines Creek strand arcs north of the McKinley strand and is also considered a combination of normal and right-lateral fault movement, juxtaposing the Pingston and Yukon-Tanana terranes.

The north-south tectonic squeeze on Alaska continues to this day. Present-day migration rates of the Pacific Plate are measured at 2.3 inches/6 centimeters per year. Mount McKinley continues to rise at an estimated rate of 0.04 inch/1 millimeter per year. As the geologic story of DNP&P continues to evolve, mountaineers will do well to plan their climbs early. The McKinley summit, and probably the neighboring peaks as well, will only get higher.

The West Buttress, although predominantly an ice and snow route, provides luring glimpses of bedrock geology along the standard course. The dominant rock involved is the McKinley granite; however, along the way climbers can frequently see Cretaceous argillite and some Foraker granite, with occasional minor peeks—pun intended—of the Nixon Fork sediments.

At base camp, views both north to Mount Frances and south to Mount Hunter are of the fifty-six-million-year-old McKinley pluton, consisting primarily of biotite granite and granodiorite (see Photo #3242, page 101). Due west at a distance of some 5 miles/8 kilometers across the Kahiltna Glacier, stands spectacular Mount Foraker, which consists of a younger, thirty-eight-million-year-old biotite and hornblende granodiorite. The dramatic relief of these peaks is basically credited to the hardness, or resistance to weathering, of the two plutons.

As the route swings out into the central Kahiltna Glacier, the 350-million-year-old Nixon Fork sediments come into view as black to brown, shaley to slatey rocks at the base of the eastern faces of Mounts Foraker and Crosson, as well as Kahiltna Dome (see Photo #4912, page 105). All three peaks are capped by Foraker granite, and the heat of the intrusion has altered or metamorphosed the sedimentary Nixon Fork rocks into hard, sometimes blocky, slates. The west ridge of west Kahiltna Peak is of argillite—approximately one hundred MYA—that has been altered by the intrusion of the McKinley granite. Both sedimentary rocks, Nixon Fork and argillite, are similar in appearance due to this alteration (see Photo #3242, page 101).

At Kahiltna Pass, contacts between the Cretaceous argillite and McKinley granite are evident. Also noticeable are broad folds in the argillite and perhaps some Nixon Fork rocks on the buttress ridge to the east of the pass. If enough snow melts, float, or loose, rocks of the contact—granite and argillite—are exposed on the ridge at about 11,000 feet/3,400 meters (see Photo #5033, page 107).

Directly above Motorcycle Hill at approximately 12,100 feet/3,700 meters, granitic rock—quartz monzonite—of the McKinley pluton is exposed and appears intermittently up to Windy Corner. Likewise, granite dominates the Basin Camp at 14,200 feet/4,300 meters, including good exposures at the Edge of the World (see Photo #5048, page 112).

At the top of the Headwall at approximately 16,200 feet/4,900 meters, granitic rock—quartz monzonite—again dominates (see Photo #6008). Within some of the ordinary quartz monzonite, light and dark banding, or veins, is identifiable. These are apilite dikes, a fine-grained, high quartz rock that may represent final crystallizing solutions that invaded joints or cracks of the precrystallized quartz monzonite. Also visible from this point is a roof pendent—a cap of argillite remaining after intrusion—on the northwest buttress.

At Denali Pass—while catching your breath—you have ample opportunity to inspect the contact between Cretaceous argillite and McKinley granite (see Photo #57-5430, page 124). In much of this area, the brownish-black argillite is highly altered to actually become hornfels, a metamorphic rock, probably by both the original granitic intrusion and subsequent dike intrusions. Jointing in the hornfels gives it its prominent slaty appearance. Float rocks and small outcrops of granite and hornfels are found intermittently as the route continues to the Football Field (see Photo #7252, page 123).

Along the final summit approach, blocks of argillite can be seen scattered along the route. From this location, the climber can turn around and see that the upper 1,500 feet/460 meters of the north peak is a large roof pendent of argillite, in near horizontal contact with the granite on the south wall of the Harper Glacier valley. Argillite bedrock is also found about 100 feet/30 meters beneath the summit of the south peak as well, demonstrating that ocean sediments are to be found at the top of the world on Denali (see Photo #7203, page 126).

Phil Brease

The Glaciers of Denali National Park and Preserve

A pproximately 16 percent of the six million acres of Denali National Park and Preserve is covered by permanent snow or ice, mostly in the form of glaciers. At one time approximately two to five million years ago, nearly the entire park was covered by an ice sheet with perhaps only a few peaks, including the upper 3,000–4,000 feet/ 900–1,200 meters of Mount McKinley, protruding from the ice. The maximum ice advance south of Denali made it all the way to Cook Inlet and Prince William Sound. At least five and perhaps as many as seven major glacial advance-recession events have occurred since this maximum ice advance, and today's glacier positions represent a significant back wasting subsequent to those major ice age advances.

Mount McKinley and the near east-west configuration of the Alaska Range form a climate barrier, creating distinctly different climate regimes on each side of the range. The south side of the range traps most of the weather systems, which generally travel from south to north, and therefore gets roughly twice as much precipitation as the north side. This difference is demonstrated by the fact that the bulk of glacier cover is on the south side of the range, with six of the seven largest glaciers in Denali being located on the south side. The seven glaciers, in order of decreasing size, are Kahiltna, Ruth, Muldrow, Eldridge, Tokositna, Yentna, and Dall. The Muldrow is the one north side representative glacier.

Because of its great height and latitudinal position, Mount McKinley is notorious for being one of the coldest mountains on earth. This exceptionally cold environment has scientific implications well beyond the obvious difficulties of survival in cold ambient temperatures. The lengthy and extremely cold winter season gives the snowpack little opportunity to warm up and consolidate, resulting in prolonged instability and constantly high avalanche danger. In most temperate zones, annual snowpack temperature gradients, even on glaciers, are fairly small. With the addition of diurnal fluctuations, the snowpack will generally move toward a more welded, consolidated mass. In northern or polar climates, the temperature gradients are large, the winter is long, and most of the year there are no significant diurnal temperature fluctuations.

These long, cold winters lead to exceptional depth, as well as surface, hoar development, resulting in less stable and unconsolidated snowpacks. Although this can and often does mean that high avalanche conditions may prevail, it also provides for earlier "springtime" snow conditions, as the snowpack, including snow bridges, tends to become rotten fast, from both the bottom and the top. These conditions make hidden crevasses perhaps the most insidious risk to the average climber on Denali.

Glacier data is scarce in Denali. In 1991, a modest data collection program began on both the Kahiltna and the Tralieka/Muldrow Glaciers, regarding mass balance, glacier flow, ice elevation changes, and other information. A single index site on the Kahiltna at the equilibrium line altitude of 5,760 feet/1,760 meters—equilibrium line altitude, or ELA, is the elevation of the glacier budget balance point, often the average late season firn line—generally indicates a negative net mass balance since installment in 1991. This means that the rate of melting exceeds the rate of precipitation. Data for the Tralieka/Muldrow system has not yet been worked up, but is expected to also show a negative balance.

Surface flow rates of a glacier vary depending on when and where the movement is measured. However, some comparisons can be made between a few glaciers in Denali. Surface flow rates for five years at the Kahiltna ELA, for instance, have averaged approximately 8 inches/45 centimeters per day since 1991, while twenty years of measurements on the Muldrow, 3 miles/5 kilometers downstream of the ELA, average just under 6 inches/15 centimeters per day. A two-day measurement on the Ruth near the 5,000-foot/1,500-meter ELA demonstrated a rapid 3 feet/1 meter of movement per day. The

Ruth probably has the highest average flow rate because it has a very large accumulation basin that must funnel down through the narrow Ruth Gorge.

Glacier behavior—size, shape, and flow characteristics—is generally most affected by climate and precipitation. However, DNP&P has more than its share of glaciers that "surge." A surging glacier is one that periodically changes its ice distribution over its length, usually resulting in more rapid flow rates, extensive crevassing, and often exceptional advancement of the terminus. Glaciers in Denali with evidence or known histories of surging include the Yentna, Dall, Tokositna, Chelodotna, Herron, Straightaway, Peters, and Muldrow. Numerous smaller, unnamed glaciers in the park have also surged at one time or another.

The Muldrow Glacier went through a surge event during 1956 and 1957. Ice elevations dropped some 300 feet/90 meters near McGonagall Pass, and surface ice velocities may have reached 1,500 feet/460 meters per day. The terminus was reported to have advanced about 4 miles/6 kilometers beyond its previous location by the time the surge ended in August 1957. Similarly, the Peters Glacier surged from midwinter 1986 to late winter 1987. The glacier terminus advanced 2.8 miles/4.5 kilometers in 291 days, probably reaching speeds of up to 336 feet/102 meters per day.

Although some of these glacier surge conditions could present new ice walls or treadmills for the climber, there is little concern for such conditions on the West Buttress route. The Kahiltna Glacier demonstrates a steady flow behavior with no indications of a surge history. Perhaps, if your timing is right, you can ascend the West Buttress and descend via the Muldrow Glacier, riding it out on its next surge!

No absolute depths are known for any of the glaciers in DNP&P. Our best—and only—information comes from a study done by K. Echelmeyer using seismic soundings right in front of Mount Dickey in the Ruth Gorge. Echelmeyer's study suggests that the ice is 3,805 feet/1,160 meters thick in the center of the glacier. Dr. Washburn notes that the distance from the summit of Mount Dickey to the bottom of the ice-filled gorge is almost 9,000 feet/2,700 meters. The gorge is 2 miles/3 kilometers wide at the top and about 1.2 miles/1.9 kilometers wide at the ice surface, making the Ruth Gorge the deepest gorge in North America. Echelmeyer points out that if the ice melted, Mount Dickey would be as big as three Yosemite El Capitans on top of each other, though not quite as steep.

A common question asked is: how deep do crevasses get? Conceivably, crevasses could go all the way down to bedrock, but most likely this is a rare occurrence. Most crevasses do not exceed one hundred feet, except on Denali where there is an abundance of crevasses deeper than this. Climbers who descended into one crevasse formed below the 14,200-foot/4,300-meter basin reported it to be over 300 feet/90 meters deep. By definition, compressional basins—usually locations of the thickest ice—are less likely to form significant crevasses, while extentional slopes, such as icefalls, are going to be areas of thinner ice accumulation.

Phil Brease

The Weather at Denali National Park and Preserve

General Conditions

*I*t is often said that the great challenge of Denali is not the climbing, but the weather. Denali is a subarctic mountain located in the middle of the southern Alaskan mainland at about sixty-three degrees north latitude which is thirty-five degrees (or approximately 2,400 miles) farther north than Everest. This is the same latitude as northern Hudson Bay and central Scandinavia. Denali's northern location means that the climate around its summit presents one of the most severe year-round averages of any spot on earth.

Denali's weather follows two different patterns: the succession of storm fronts which pass over the peak referred to as "upslope flow," and storms generated by the mountain itself. These patterns are typical of all the great mountains of the world, but are pronounced on Denali because the mountain rises, almost completely isolated, to an altitude of 20,320 feet/6,190 meters out of level lowlands. It is also located only 130 miles/210 kilometers from tidewater at the head of Cook Inlet and therefore receives, without obstruction, the full force of the coastal storms that pass its way. The one weather phenomenon seldom observed on Denali is lightning.

Most of the weather flows from the Bering Sea to the west and southwest, and from the Gulf of Alaska and the North Pacific to the south. Bering Sea storms are typically windy while North Pacific storms out of the south bring large amounts of precipitation. The faster the winds are aloft and the farther south the origin of the flow, the worse the weather. These southwesters are preceded by the usual warnings of a warm front: high cirrus clouds, increasing winds, and falling barometric pressure. Usually about twelve hours pass from the time the first 30,000-foot/9,000-meter cirrus streamer appears until the peak is actually enveloped in overcast and precipitation begins. Despite the adverse weather caused by fronts, their danger is lessened by their more predictable character and the forewarning they provide to the alert climber. During the spring and early summer climbing season, temperatures fluctuate dramatically over a 24-hour period. This is especially true in valley sites such as Kahiltna Base Camp where it may drop below 0°F at night and rise to the 40s during the midday sun. Variation of temperature is less on exposed ridges and on the route above 16,200 feet/4,900 meters.

Localized storms on Denali often take the form of lenticular cloud caps. The ambient air around Denali is naturally warmer during the summer months than the mountain itself. The air is also likely to be relatively moist. If the wind loft is 20–50 miles/30–80 kilometers per hour, this air, when it hits the peak and streams up over and around it, creates a lenticular cloud cap that rapidly varies in size and tendency to precipitate depending on the temperature and humidity of the air mass. Storms of this sort, while the entire region about the peak is cloudless, can appear or disappear with incredible swiftness—within fifteen to twenty minutes—and often bring fierce blizzards of short duration. These storms typically clear away in the evening when the air around the mountain chills.

From 1983 to 1996, the National Weather Service collected weather data from the 7,200-foot/2,200-meter and 14,200-foot/4,300-meter camps on the West Buttress during May, June, and the first week of July. Research revealed that large-scale weather patterns could be accurately forecasted a couple days in advance, but local

A particularly fierce lenticular cloud on Mount Foraker.
©Brian Okonek

weather remained highly unpredictable. Some interesting patterns surfaced that may help the climber in the difficult art of Denali forecasting.

Specific Patterns

A *west to southwest* flow pattern brings Bering Sea storms into the area which usually last four days. Both strong wind and heavy snow normally result.

A *northwest* flow pattern puts Denali downwind from much of the Alaska Interior. The large number of small lakes, ponds, and muskeg swamps in the Interior become a significant source of moisture. Remnants of thunderstorms easily get trapped in Kahiltna Pass and poor weather funnels down the Kahiltna.

A *north to northeast* flow pattern brings clear weather, but strong winds, for a couple of days.

East to southeast is a common flow pattern indicative of changeable weather. Lenticulars will form and dissipate unpredictably for a week or more.

A common weather observation reported by climbers is cloud tops to 11,000 feet/3,400 meters, with mostly clear skies above and a lenticular barring the way to the summit.

Between upslope flow and weather fronts, the portion of Denali above 12,000 feet/3,700 meters has very little clear weather, and periods of clear, calm weather near the summit rarely exceed twelve hours. Given this, the important forecasting objective for the climber is to determine the trend of any given storm passing through: is it improving or worsening? The answer to this question should be the main determinant for whether to climb or stay put.

Climbers may call the National Weather Service in Fairbanks at any hour to speak directly with a weather forecaster at 907-456-0372 or 907-456-0373.

Ted Fathauer

Wildlife

*N*o official research on flora and fauna has been conducted above snow line on Denali. Tree line is only 2,000 feet/600 meters and vegetation extends to approximately 4,000 feet/1,200 meters. Mosses are found only up to about 5,500 feet/1,700 meters and then only on warm, sunny south slopes. Pilots and climbers have painted a picture of what sorts of animals frequent the mountain and have noted some impressive animal adventures. Being far above tree line, however, the West Buttress is quite a lifeless world. Nevertheless, a few species have eked out a niche for themselves.

Cunning, mischievous, and playful ravens frequent the West Buttress, taking advantage of unwary climbers. They excavate poorly cached food supplies and entertain stormbound climbers with aerobatics over wind-blasted ridges as high as Denali Pass at 18,200 feet/ 5,500 meters. Shy and cautious, they seldom venture into camps when anyone is around. Besides climbers' food, ravens often scavenge the dead bodies of birds that have been unable to make their migration over the Alaska Range. Scattered feathers on the glacier are all that remain of them.

Many birds cross the Alaska Range on their migrations to the Interior. A variety of song birds, including Juncos, tree swallows, Wilson warblers, fox sparrows, red-winged blackbirds, shorebirds, raptors, and waterfowl, are typically seen in May. Sandhill cranes can be seen in the fall. Owls have even been observed crossing over the mountains. Large Vs of Canadian geese and trumpeter swans often use the Kahiltna Glacier and Pass as a route to their northern nesting grounds. Even during whiteouts, they can be heard honking and trumpeting as they travel through the range. Snow buntings have been spotted as high as 19,300 feet/5,900 meters. Gray-crowned rosy finches frequent Kahiltna Base Camp. They apparently nest in the nearby rocky cliffs, and in July fledglings noisily compete for food from the parents in camp. It is common to have weakened, disoriented birds show up in camp seeking shelter among the bright colors.

A common merganzer became grounded on the upper Kahiltna Glacier one spring. Despite desperate attempts to take off, leaving long sets of tracks and wing beats in the powdery snow, the duck was unable to get itself airborne. A descending climber captured the tired bird, hauled it to base camp, and then flew it to Talkeetna with one of the air services. The liberated bird spent a good deal of the summer in a pond near town.

The nasal chirps of the pika, a 5-ounce/145-gram rodent, have been heard among the rocks at the base of Mount Frances. Ermine tracks were seen in the same vicinity. Wolverine tracks have also been found near Kahiltna Base, and a black bear was spotted at the southeast fork of the Kahiltna Glacier. At this elevation on the Kahiltna Glacier there are approximately eight miles to firn line and twenty miles to any significant vegetation.

At the base of Mount Huntington, above a horrendous icefall of the Tokositna Glacier, two climbers were chased out of their camp by a thin and obviously hungry black bear. The bear proceeded to ravage their supplies and then slept in the debris while the climbers watched and shivered all night in their underwear nearby! A remarkable sighting of a grizzly bear was made after an extended storm in 1994. Two climbers came across the bear above Windy Corner at 13,600 feet/4,100 meters, as they descended the mountain. The bear ran off and fell into a crevasse, never to be seen again. A loose sled dog once fell into a crevasse in the same area and was presumed dead. Two weeks later the dog showed up at the 14,200-foot/4,300-meter Basin Camp—hungry, but otherwise no worse for the wear.

Perhaps the oddest animal encounter was with a red squirrel begging for food at 12,500 feet/3,800 meters. This is no less than 15 miles/24 kilometers and over 10,000 feet/3,000 meters in elevation from the nearest spruce grove. Did the little mammal arrive on the glacier in someone's duffel in a gorp-induced coma?

The unexpected presence of animals on Denali provides a welcome addition to what sometimes seems like an unrelieved panorama of blue ice and white snow.

Brian Okonek

A History of Denali Rescues

*T*he National Park Service's high altitude mountain rescue capabilities are on the cutting edge of the rescue business. With few locations imitating Denali's diversely hazardous environment, climbing rangers have had to pioneer their own systems and philosophy of rescue management. The risk and concern for the rescuer is high, as is the desire to help the fallen climber. The NPS's approach to managing rescues has changed over time with the different styles of superintendents, increased experience of rangers, advancements in rescue technology, and available funds.

The expense, responsibility, and risk associated with a rescue on Denali have been major management issues since the early days of the park. In 1932, the first season in which expeditions on Mount McKinley were administered by the NPS, accidents, deaths, a body recovery, and a rescue occurred. One of the expeditions was made up of NPS officials. Harry Liek, the park's second superintendent, Grant Pearson, a park ranger who later would become superintendent, and two others made the second ascent of both the south and north summits of Denali via the Muldrow Glacier. Park officials experienced firsthand the seriousness of Denali's cold, glaciated slopes. All members suffered some degree of frostbite. Pearson caught a crampon and fell while descending from the summit, and later fell unroped forty feet into a crevasse, miraculously surviving with only minor scrapes.

While Liek's team was high on the mountain, the Cosmic Ray expedition flew onto the Muldrow Glacier, making the first glacier ski plane landing. It was also the first time in which two expeditions were on the mountain simultaneously. Liek's party, anticipating a happy reunion while descending the mountain, found that tragedy had befallen the other expedition. Allen Carpé, one of the most accomplished mountaineers of the day, had disappeared in a crevasse fall and presumably died. Koven's body was found on the glacier and a third member was seriously ill at base camp, requiring rescue. The NPS learning curve on conducting rescues was steep right from the beginning.

From 1940 to the late 1960s, the NPS rescue philosophy on avoiding accidents focused on screening climbers. NPS wanted to stay out of the rescue business. Rangers interviewed climbers in an effort to know the ability and experience level of the group, and personally checked climbers' equipment to ensure adequacy in an arctic environment. Only after passing this test could climbers receive approval by the superintendent and be granted permission to climb. However, with limited resources available for rescue, expeditions were required to have a standby expedition ready to go to their assistance in case of an emergency. The Alaska Mountain Rescue Group out of Anchorage accepted responsibility for many expeditions and were also authorized by the National Park Service to do the required equipment checks. Another group from Fairbanks, the Alpine Rescue Unit of Alaska, also volunteered their services.

The U.S. Air Force Rescue Coordination Center and Alaska Air Command provided logistical expertise and air support in order to further the NPS's rescue capabilities. As harder routes were climbed, the Alaska Mountain Rescue Group decided to be on standby only for expeditions attempting the "easier" routes. They were concerned about exposing their volunteers to the higher risks associated with the more difficult climbs being pioneered.

The NPS's strategies for managing safety-related issues in the park continued to evolve, and inevitably stirred controversy among climbers. In 1950, Superintendent Grant Pearson was compelled to declare, "The Park Service is not trying to prevent people from climbing mountains in this park, but is trying to make it as safe as possible and prevent accidents. If trouble develops while climbing in this park, which it has before, it is our duty to do everything possible to go to their rescue." By the late 1960s, the expenses related to rescuing climbers had grown into an important issue and there was already talk of requiring climbers to carry rescue insurance. In 1968, the state legislature introduced a bill requiring bonding of climbing parties, but the bill was not passed. The cost of rescuing climbers, although relatively small compared to rescuing lost hunters or downed airplane pilots, was growing and receiving regular attention from the news media.

In 1972, after conducting one of the earliest high altitude helicopter rescue on the mountain, U.S. Air Force Lieutenant General Sherril wrote to Stanley Albright of the NPS, "The natural humanitarian instincts to help must be carefully balanced with the risks inherent in committing an air crew and helicopter to the extreme limits of their operational capability." He went on to say that the military would not compete with civilian helicopters for rescues if the latter were available. Civilian helicopters were not always available, nor were many companies eager to send their equipment and crews to Denali. The NPS's ability to conduct efficient, timely, and safe rescue operations became more compromised on account of delays spent looking for suitable aircraft and assembling a team of rescuers. The NPS, despite its resistance to involvement, found itself forced into the rescue business in order to better protect the park's climbing visitors. By the mid-1970s, the NPS seasonal staff included skilled

Mountaineering ranger Daryl Miller, middle front, and his patrol. ©Mark Elstad

climbing rangers hired to help execute rescue operations. To this day, climbing patrols include some of the United States' strongest climbers: John Roskelley, Mark Twight, Scott Backes, Pete Athans, Mark Wilford, and Alex Lowe, and some of the most knowledgeable climbers/medical professionals, including Colin Grissom, Larry Hamilton, Jim Litch, and Buck Tilton.

By 1991, problems in procuring military or civilian helicopters to perform rescue work led the NPS to begin leasing a French-made, high altitude Lama helicopter for the climbing season. Alouette in

Talkeetna has allowed pilots and NPS mountaineering patrols to train together and be available at short notice, which has added greatly to the safety of the rescue teams and their efficiency when responding to emergencies throughout DNP&P. In 1993, during a training exercise, pilot Bill "Cowboy" Ramsey flew the Lama with NPS mountaineering ranger Daryl Miller dangling from a 100-foot/30-meter rope to Denali's summit, thus completing the world's highest

Every lost climber represents a tragedy. ©*Mark Elstad*

"short haul." Increased rescue capabilities are not without the help of the U.S. Army Northern Warfare Unit, the Air National Guard, the various Talkeetna air services, and other climbers and guides on the mountain.

Brian Okonek

Frostbite and Altitude-related Illnesses

*T*he high altitude and harsh environment of Denali, combined with the large number of climbers on the mountain results in numerous altitude and cold-related health problems. From May to June, temperatures at the 14,200–17,200-foot/4,300–5,200-meter level reach -20°F to -40°F at night, and storms with winds of fifty to one hundred miles per hour can last for several days. The northern latitude results in the barometric pressure on Denali being lower for a given altitude than on mountains closer to the equator. This difference becomes noticeable above 10,000 feet/3,000 meters and makes the summit of Denali physiologically equivalent to most 21,000–23,000-foot/6,400–7,000-meter peaks. Many climbers, including those with Himalayan experience, are unprepared for this harsh mountain environment.

Frostbite
Frostbite is a cold injury, usually localized, that is characterized by the freezing of body tissue. The tissue may die as a result of inadequate circulation. The first signs of frostbite are numbness, poor capillary refill, and a white, waxy, and wooden texture to the skin.

In 1985 my partner and I were high on the Cassin Ridge at 17,000 feet/5,200 meters, planning to summit the next day. We were excited that all the hard climbing was behind us and that soon we would be safely down on the West Buttress. Within twelve hours, however, a ferocious storm was upon us with winds blowing so hard it sounded like a freight train passing by. We stayed put for four days until the wind died down and safely made the summit without frostbite. A pair of Dutch climbers also on the Cassin climbed through the storm, bivouacked on the summit, and descended to 14,200 feet on the West Buttress. They were off the mountain sooner than us, but not without frostbitten faces and fingers resulting in permanent damage and loss of tissue. A little patience can often make the difference between permanent injury and just another stormbound climbing story.

Many factors contribute to frostbite, including inadequate equipment, impatience, and neglect. Most cases of frostbite of the hands or feet occur on days when climbers would have been better off staying in their tents. The wind, in particular, is often the villain. Blowing cold, dry air results in convective heat loss, but it also dehydrates and exhausts climbers, making them more susceptible to frostbite. On summit day, a typical frostbite victim uses gloves instead of mittens, supergaiters instead of overboots, and leaves camp in 30–50-mile-/50–80-kilometer-per-hour winds.

Unlucky victims who frostbite their fingers or toes can take some measures to improve healing and prevent further damage. The preferred treatment is rapid rewarming in a sterile water bath at 100°F–108°F. On Denali, however, most climbers with cases of frostbite are passively rewarmed in the sleeping bag before they arrive back at Kahiltna Base. During descent, the affected extremity should be kept warm, clean, and dry. Constrictive clothing that might impair circulation to the extremity, as well as additional refreezing or trauma, should be avoided. Hands should be wrapped with a loose gauze dressing and insulated with mittens. Toes and feet pose a particular challenge because after being wrapped in a gauze dressing, they need to go back into boots for the descent. Inner boots may need to be cut to allow for more room. Great care should be taken not to break blisters while in the field. Most important is preventing the affected extremity from being refrozen. Other measures that help the frostbite victim include staying well hydrated and warm, and taking 800 milligrams of ibuprofen every 8 hours to decrease inflammation. All frostbite cases should be evaluated by a physician as soon as possible after flying off the mountain.

Seldom heard from frostbite victims are their accounts of the months and years they spend in painful rehabilitation. Victims with severely frostbitten fingers on both hands cannot feed or wash themselves, or wipe their own bottoms for months. They are forever sensitive to the cold, and vulnerable to further injury. Some are forced to quit mountaineering and relocate to a warmer environment, such as Florida. Getting frostbitten is a big deal!

Prevention is always easier than treatment when it comes to frostbite or any injury, especially on Denali. Wearing adequate clothing, staying well hydrated, and avoiding exposure to extreme conditions are infinitely preferable to dealing with even minor frostbite on the descent and after the expedition.

Altitude-related Illnesses

Illnesses caused by high altitude range from uncomfortable problems to dangerous conditions and are all related to the decreased oxygen concentration in the blood caused by the lower atmospheric pressure found at higher elevations. The common denominator behind most of the resultant problems is edema: the swelling and pooling of body fluid. When this occurs in the brain or lungs, the results can be devastating.

Acute Mountain Sickness (AMS) and High Altitude Cerebral Edema (HACE)

We were climbing unroped on the steep terrain near the top of the West Rib of Denali. We had made good progress initially after an early morning start from our high camp at 16,000 feet/4,900 meters, but the higher we climbed the slower we moved. I took comfort from my four partners, who were leaning on their ice axes and panting every few steps, because I was doing the same with increasing frequency. About a week had passed since we started up the initial couloir that gained the West Rib from the head of the northeast fork of the Kahiltna, and we were all feeling the effects of the altitude. As we neared the summit plateau at 19,000 feet/5,800 meters, I noticed that one member of our expedition was starting to stagger; by the time we reached the easier terrain on the summit plateau he was slurring his speech and complaining of a headache. Clearly he couldn't go on. We stopped to help him into a sleeping bag. He felt nauseous and began to vomit. After resting awhile and sipping on a hot drink he was able to descend the

West Buttress with us, and subsequently recovered uneventfully after a
night's rest several thousand feet lower down on the mountain.
The above scenario occurred on my first trip to Denali in 1982.
I often reflect back on the experience and wonder what we would
have done if we had not been able to descend. Unaware to us at the
time, the ill member of our group had severe acute mountain sickness (AMS) that was progressing to high altitude cerebral edema
(HACE). If we had not been able to descend because of bad weather,
or because he had become incapacitated, the outcome might have
been tragic.

AMS is the most common form of altitude illness and is seen a
few hours to a few days after ascent to altitudes of over 8,300 feet/
2,500 meters. Symptoms include headache, dizziness, decreased
appetite, nausea, difficulty sleeping, and decreased energy. Swelling of the hands and feet and around the eyes caused by fluid retention are also common signs. Mild AMS usually resolves itself within
a couple of days at the same elevation. Severe AMS causes victims
to lose their balance and walk as if they were drunk, a condition
called ataxia. This is due to increased swelling in the brain and is
essentially a progression to HACE.

High altitude cerebral edema should be suspected in any individual whose level of consciousness deteriorates or who is acting
in an abnormal or irrational manner. A victim of HACE will not be
able to walk in a straight line. Within hours, HACE progresses from
drowsiness to coma, and ultimately death. Immediate descent to
a lower altitude is imperative for survival. Oxygen is helpful, if
available, but is not a substitute for descent. Dexamethasone
(Decadron) is also helpful at a dose of 4 milligrams by mouth or
injected intramuscularly every 6 hours.

Gradual ascent and speedy descent are the best ways to prevent or treat altitude illnesses, but pharmacological options also
exist which may help in some cases. Acetazolamide (Diamox), the
drug of choice for treating AMS, works by stimulating breathing and
thus improving the oxygen level in the blood. Some climbers start
taking Diamox at Kahiltna Base; however, the side effect of increased
urination resulting in dehydration leads many to take it only after
the onset of AMS. A dose of 125–250 milligrams twice a day is

recommended. Once taken, Diamox should be continued during the ascent, but may be stopped after one or two days at the same altitude. Upon further ascent, it may be restarted. At higher altitudes, many climbers take 125 milligrams of Diamox prior to going to bed to prevent periodic, or irregular, breathing. Diamox should not be taken by those allergic to sulfa drugs.

Anyone needing to take Decadron, which is used to treat HACE, should consider descending immediately. Decadron is a steroid and may cause many of the side effects of this class of drugs, including depression or euphoria, bizarre dreams, and fluid retention. Decadron is not an anabolic steroid, the kind used by some athletes to enhance performance. Unlike Diamox, the use of Decadron for more than a few days at a time is not recommended because of more serious long-term effects of the drug, which include weight gain, decreased bone density, and impaired wound healing. Decadron is an option for treating serious AMS in those individuals allergic to sulfa drugs. The dose is 4 milligrams every 6–8 hours.

Given how little is known about altitude illnesses, taking medication to prevent its occurrence or as a treatment should be decided upon only after careful consideration.

High Altitude Pulmonary Edema (HAPE)

I awoke from a restless night's sleep in the well-sheltered camp we had placed on a platform in the bergschrund below Windy Corner, an exposed area at 13,000 feet/4,000 meters on the West Buttress. I felt weak and tired, as if I had the flu. As we packed up camp I was breathing a lot harder than usual. Just shouldering my heavy pack was an ordeal, and we didn't get too far out of camp that morning before my partners had to take the bulk of my load. The climber's camp at 14,200 feet/4,300 meters on Denali was only a few hours away, but at the rate I was moving it would take us most of the day to get there. As we moved higher I had to stop more frequently because of coughing episodes, and to allow myself to gasp for more air. I was young and fit, and I had HAPE.

HAPE is a condition in which the tiny air sacs in the lungs, called alveoli, fill with fluid, a condition which impairs the diffusion of oxygen from the lungs to the blood. As my own case illustrates, HAPE is characterized by an increased shortness of breath both at rest and with exercise, and a dry cough that progresses to a cough producing pink, frothy sputum. A climbing partner who is moving slower than usual, breathing with more difficulty, and coughing may be developing HAPE. As the lung fluid increases, the affected individual may be able to walk only short distances before needing to rest, and gurgling may be heard when you place your ear against the chest wall. A purplish discoloration of the lips and fingernails caused by a low oxygen level in the blood may also be observed. Death may occur within hours if HAPE is left untreated.

The best treatment for HAPE is early recognition and descent to a lower altitude. At the first indication that HAPE is developing, descent should be undertaken while the individual can still walk, rappel, or down climb under his or her own power. Descent of as few as two or three thousand feet usually results in marked improvements. Oxygen, if available, is also an effective treatment for HAPE; usually the individual requires only 3–4 liters of oxygen per minute via nasal cannula. A portable hyperbaric chamber (Gamow™ bag) is also effective treatment for HAPE, but should not be used as a substitute for descent. When an ill climber comes out of a Gamow™ bag, he or she is still at the same altitude and HAPE may continue to progress. Gamow™ bags and oxygen are most useful when descent must be delayed because of weather or terrain.

Although various effective treatment options for high altitude illnesses exist, there are no miracle remedies. Researchers continue to study and attempt to understand why some people acclimate to altitude and others do not. HACE and HAPE afflicts the strong and weak alike, although being aerobically fit provides a definite advantage. The best prevention of high altitude sickness is avoidance via a gradual ascent allowing time for acclimatization and special attention to the early signs of development. Limit the rate of ascent to 1,000–2,000 feet/300–600 meters per day. Alpine-style ascents should include a prolonged acclimatization period, seven to ten days at 14,200 feet/4,300 meters beforehand. When altitude illnesses do occur, descent is always the most effective treatment. In mild cases of AMS, an extra night or two at the same elevation usually provides enough time to adjust. In the words of wilderness medicine guru Buck Tilton, "Successful prevention of illness and injury from cold and high altitude follows the same basic guidelines as achieving a successful climb: you make careful plans, and you carefully follow your plans."

Colin Grissom, M.D.

Women's Concerns

*D*enali's West Buttress provides an incredible mountaineering experience for over a thousand climbers each year, of which only 5–7 percent are women. Most of these women are from outside the United States, which makes the West Buttress an especially exciting place in which to see and meet female mountaineers from around the world.

Women climbing Denali need to be aware of certain medical and practical concerns which may affect the success of their climb. Much of the following information is based on common sense but bears mentioning as a reminder of what women can expect in Denali's extreme environment.

In an effort to minimize the inconvenience of urinating during the climb, some women drink less water, thus becoming more susceptible to dehydration. In order to avoid this dangerous health risk, women simply need to accept the inconvenience of having to expend more energy on this normal bodily function in order to stay properly hydrated. There are, however, certain techniques and equipment that decrease the laboriousness of urinating on the climb. During the day, a proper climbing harness and clothing system will allow women to urinate easily while staying tied into the rope. At night, urinating into a wide-mouthed bottle or a heavy plastic bag alleviates the chore of having to exit the tent during a storm; if placed outside the tent, the bag will be frozen by morning. Another strategy for both trail and tent is the use of a "pee funnel," which allows women to urinate in an upright position. These techniques require experimentation and practice at home well before the date of the climb, as their effectiveness varies from individual to individual. The abrupt change in environment and physical activity, as well as the length of a Denali expedition, can radically affect the menstrual cycle. Women should expect their periods to change in some way. Menstruation may start off schedule or not at all, occur twice in a month, or with a different amount of flow. It pays to be prepared; even the most experienced female mountaineers get caught off guard!

One solution to menstrual irregularity on a wilderness expedition is to use oral or injected contraceptives. At high altitude, however, taking these contraceptives may cause the development of blood clots in the legs, a condition known as deep venous thrombosis. Although women are not at risk of developing blood clots while using these contraceptives at sea level (nonsmokers, that is), the risk has not been well studied at high altitude. Therefore, most experts recommend that these contraceptives not be used by women during high altitude exposure. Women already taking birth control pills or Depro-Prevera before ascending to high altitude should consult a doctor familiar with altitude-related problems about the added risks of blood clotting, excessive edema, and other health problems.

Because of the potential for irregular menstrual bleeding at high altitude and/or during an expedition, women are susceptible to anemia. Anemia can adversely affect exercise performance because it decreases the oxygen-carrying capacity of the blood. Therefore, supplemental iron should be taken daily during a strenuous high altitude expedition. In addition, it is a good idea for women to have their blood tested before the expedition to be sure that they are not anemic; 120 days before the expedition will allow adequate time to replete iron stores and correct anemia.

While on any extended backcountry expedition, women are especially prone to developing yeast and urinary tract infections (UTIs). To decrease the likelihood of becoming infected, women should pay particular attention to keeping the genital area clean. Some suggestions are: use moist towelettes at least once a day, wear cotton underpants, and use toilet paper, or the equivalent, to dry off after urinating. "Holding it" while on a rope team is thought to promote UTIs. Choose a harness with leg loops that drop away and a combination of clothes that makes access as easy as possible. Talk to your doctor about specific antibiotics for bladder and yeast infections to add to the expedition's medical kit.

For most women, it is important to have some sense of privacy, especially when roped together or sharing a tent and camp with a bunch of men. You can make it clear that the guys need to turn around when you are urinating while on a rope team. The camp latrine can be built in such a way that the wind walls offer some privacy.

A small stuff sack is handy to carry as a "toilet bag" for tampons or sanitary napkins and towelettes; carry an empty plastic bag for waste.

Caitlin Palmer

When to Climb

*T*he most commonly asked question by climbers is: which is the best month in which to climb? There really is no right answer as every year is different from the one before. It is generally agreed that the practical climbing season on Denali begins in late April and lasts through the end of July, shrinking the acceptable window of climbing time to ninety days. In March and April, cold temperatures and strong winds at higher elevations make conditions severe for climbing. May is colder than June and cold weather is less prone to snowfall, but Denali tends to defy meteorological rules. Arguably the best month in which to climb is July for the mildest and most stable weather and long hours of daylight. However, July sees fewer climbers because of the very real threat of having to walk back to Talkeetna if planes cannot land at 7,200 feet/2,200 meters due to deteriorating snow conditions. The National Park Service currently forbids landings higher up on the Kahiltna, where the snow remains suitable through the end of July. Precipitation and poor weather frequent August, and by late in that month, lasting snowfall signals the arrival of another winter.

There really is no best month to climb Denali. Luck will play a big part, and plenty of time, food, and fuel to wait out storms will greatly enhance your chance of reaching the summit.

Winter Ascent

A winter ascent of the West Buttress borders on suicidal," asserts Alaska Range climber and mountaineering ranger, Roger Robinson. It is definitely not for just anyone. The coldest weather on Denali is from November to mid-April with temperatures at 19,000 feet/5,800 meters ranging from -30°F to -70°F. The jet stream, at 100+ miles per hour/160+ kilometers per hour, will often descend over the mountain's upper flanks, successfully bottoming out any thermometer. Add the dimension of Alaska's winter darkness and you get a picture of one of the most inhospitable places on earth. Dave Johnston, Art Davidson, and Ray Genet made the first winter ascent in March, 1967. Davidson's account, "Minus 148°," is a testament to the severity of the climb. Anyone thinking of climbing Denali in winter should first climb it during the summer to become familiarized with the route and get a vague idea of what conditions might be like.

Grade and Difficulty of the West Buttress Route

A s a grade II, the West Buttress shares with the Muldrow route the status of having the lowest grade on Denali, thus offering the easiest and safest route to the summit. Relative to other climbs on Denali, the West Buttress is easier and the terrain fairly moderate. But it is still Denali, which is never easy. Unique to Denali's rating system is an implied severity grade which makes any route a serious undertaking. High altitude, extreme weather, and active glaciers combine to make Denali one of the most difficult and deadly mountains in the world to climb, regardless of the grade.

Is Denali for You?

According to NPS statistics, since 1903, approximately 50 percent of all of Denali's climbers reach the summit. The challenge facing those who climb the West Buttress is primarily one of perseverance. Most climbers who fail to make it to the top underestimate the effects of cold and altitude, as well as the sheer amount of work involved, and run out of energy or motivation. The day-to-day effort of forging ahead, building camp, and dealing with hazards is mentally draining and requires a strong work ethic. Denali is no place to begin learning about winter camping and how to travel on a glacier. Rather, it should be the final exam after a long apprenticeship elsewhere.

People get badly hurt or die on the West Buttress every year. Accidents happen to climbers of all ability levels, on technical and nontechnical terrain, in good and bad weather, low on the mountain

Denali's summit ridge. ©Brian Okonek

and at high altitude, ascending and descending. Sometimes it is due to bad luck, but most of the time an accident boils down to a climber underestimating the mountain or overestimating his or her abilities in a rush for the summit. A variety of factors, including extensive travel on highly crevassed glaciers, extreme cold, inclement weather, exposed third class terrain, highly variable snow conditions, high altitude, long duration of climbs, and fatigue, combine to make Denali a uniquely dangerous place. These different elements often combine to dull both physical and mental prowess, making even relatively easy terrain deadly. Case histories of accidents show a pattern of recurring mistakes. Names such as Autobahn and Orient Express have been given to snow slopes in deference to the repeated falls down them. A safe mentality on Denali is one highly tuned to hazards and the early signs of trouble.

West Buttress climbers should be practiced and prepared to deal with certain situations: extricating another climber from a crevasse, lowering an incapacitated individual down an icy headwall, stabilizing a broken leg, short-roping an ataxic climber along a narrow ridge, stabilizing someone while digging in and camping until weather conditions improve. More insidious, but just as lethal and quite often the underlying cause for many accidents, are the effects of fatigue, dehydration, hypothermia, frostbite, and altitude-related illnesses. It is imperative to be on the lookout for any condition that might reduce judgment and endurance.

Those individuals unsure of their climbing ability can sign up with a class specifically designed to teach and evaluate mountaineering skills relative to climbing the West Buttress. Contact the NPS in Talkeetna for references.

Accident Prevention

*R*egardless of your motivation for climbing and the amount of risk you are willing to take, it is important to climb with experience backing each decision. Do not let the popular West Buttress route, with its gregarious social scene, lull you into complacency.

Climb as if yours were the only expedition on the mountain. Know and use proper techniques for safe glacier travel and climbing. Probe carefully for potential crevasses before coming together and unroping on any glacier. Do not camp someplace merely because someone else did. Look around and make sure you are safe from objective hazards. Have patience with the weather and altitude; wait out storms or acclimatize before pushing on. Many steps can be taken to minimize the risks of climbing in this environment and it is every climber's responsibility to do so.

It would be wishful thinking to believe that an accident could not befall your expedition. It is important to be prepared for the "what ifs" in mountaineering. If an accident occurs, it will be necessary to choose the simplest, most efficient, and safest techniques to perform the rescue tasks with the resources available. Carrying survival and emergency gear with you at all times will greatly assist you in handling an emergency. Practicing rescue scenarios beforehand that are pertinent to the unique mountaineering environment of Denali offers a vital link to your team's self-sufficiency and safety. Do not rely on help to be available, your radio to work, or an NPS helicopter to be able to fly you out if an accident befalls your team.

The majority of climbing accidents on Denali occur on the descent. ©Daryl Miller

A more realistic accident scenario includes your team only, with the gear in your packs and the knowledge in your heads to perform the lifesaving measures needed to rescue yourselves. Climbers must be self-sufficient with their skills and equipment, and maintain the necessary attitude that they can take care of their own problems.

When summoned, NPS climbing rangers will first talk to the party having trouble and ascertain if the climbers can help themselves rather then send out a rescue mission immediately. The NPS may also choose to provide equipment to assist in the rescue rather than pull someone off the mountain by helicopter. They will encourage each party to be as self-reliant as possible.

Brian Okonek

Emergency Evacuation

*D*epending upon the seriousness of the injury or illness, the weather, and the location of the incident, accident victims may need assistance for evacuation from other climbers, guides, mountaineering rangers, fixed-wing airplanes, or helicopters.

It is highly recommended that your party carry a radio for emergency situations. Communication becomes a vital link in any rescue that needs the assistance of more people, expertise, or equipment than your party alone can provide. Be sure to carry spare batteries and keep them warm. Through a chain of relayed messages, you may eventually communicate with NPS climbing rangers. They will want to know your registered group name, your location and elevation, the number of people needing assistance, the severity of illness or injury, weather conditions, how much food and fuel you have, and how many climbers, if any, are available to assist you with your plan of action. Speak in a normal voice, slowly and concisely. If while calling out you do not receive an answer, broadcast your message in the blind. It is possible that your radio's receiver is not functioning properly. Non-English-speaking climbers should say, "Rescue, rescue" and attempt to relay the above information in English, and then repeat the message in their own language. They should repeat the message several times, speaking as slowly and clearly as possible.

Anyone involved in a rescue situation who does not have the benefit of radio communication will have to rely heavily on their mountaineering experience, rescue practice, and ingenuity to either keep themselves safe or aid others in trouble. The universal distress symbols for ground-to-aircraft communication are a large, contrasting X made on the snow or standing with both arms raised straight above your head. A signal mirror can add dramatically to your chances of being seen from the air. Remember that despite bright clothing you will be but a tiny speck on a gigantic mountain.

Rescues put a lot of people at risk when dealing with poor snow conditions, exposed slopes, changing weather, and altitude. Some storms make it impossible for rescuers to move on the ground, let alone in the air. The selfless assistance provided by climbers through the years has saved countless lives, but not without hardships and aborted climbs for the rescue volunteers. Once a rescue is called for there is absolutely no guarantee that it is going to happen immediately or even within a couple of days; the mountain is too big and remote and the weather too unpredictable. The human instinct to help an injured person drives many an adrenaline-pumped rescuer to climb or fly in conditions in which prudence would dictate another course of action. It does the victim no good if the rescuers become injured. Rescuers must weigh all the factors carefully and proceed with great caution.

Brian Okonek

Getting There

*T*he seaport of Anchorage, Alaska, with its sea level elevation, is the usual starting point for McKinley expeditions. Anchorage is Alaska's largest city, with 258,000 residents, almost half the state's population. As the headquarters for Prudhoe Bay oil companies, it has prospered to become the center of the state's commerce and financial communities. First impressions are based on the appearance of uncontrolled urban sprawl with seemingly countless numbers of strip malls and warehouse stores. Closer inspection reveals a city majestically located next to the impressive Chugach Mountains.

Getting to Anchorage incurs the largest expense for most expeditions, whether arriving from the Lower 48 or a foreign country, all of which is referred to as "Outside" by Alaska residents. Coming from "America," another affectionate term for the Lower 48, there are three choices of travel: by road, sea, or plane. Coming from Asia or Europe, most airlines have dropped their direct flight over the North Pole to Anchorage and passengers must first fly to a gateway city such as Los Angeles, Seattle, or Vancouver to pick up a second flight to Anchorage.

Flying

Hundreds of flights arrive daily at Anchorage International Airport. Airfares fluctuate wildly; it is wise to shop around. Bargain fares exist, but are usually restrictive. The cheapest fares are the $80–$100 one-way tickets to and from Seattle offered by travel agents in Seattle and Anchorage. Most airlines have baggage restrictions which limit passengers to two or three duffels weighing 70 pounds/32 kilograms each, and strictly prohibit carrying aboard fuel of any type. Bags may be stored at the airport for a nominal daily fee.

A public bus, the People Mover, transports people from the airport to downtown Anchorage, but its schedule is somewhat erratic. Also available are numerous hotel shuttle buses and taxis. Taxis to downtown Anchorage cost $10–$15, depending upon traffic. A popular option is to arrange to have a Talkeetna taxi service meet you at the airport (see Appendix D).

Driving

There is one highway connecting the Lower 48 and Canada to central Alaska: the Alaska-Canada Highway. The "Al-Can" is paved and maintained gravel, with service stations well placed along the way. The week-long drive from Seattle of 2,435 miles/3,918 kilometers is an adventure in itself. It is well to know ahead of time that gas costs almost twice the price in Canada. It is wise to bring two spare tires.

Ferry Service

The ferry to Alaska is an unforgettable scenic wildlife experience, albeit an expensive one. Ferries to Alaska leave from Bellingham, Washington and Prince Rupert, British Columbia and travel to Haines, Alaska via the Inside Passage, an ocean route protected by islands in the U.S. and Canada. There is no connecting ferry service across the Gulf of Alaska to Anchorage because of the danger of exposure to storms from the open sea. The driving distance from Haines to Anchorage is 750 miles/1,210 kilometers. The ferry ticket for a vehicle with one passenger costs $736 one way, and $240 for passenger only. The ferry usually leaves once a week from each port. Reservations are strongly advised during the summer and can be made by contacting the Alaska Marine Highway, P.O. Box 25535, Juneau, AK 99802-5345; 800-642-0066.

Customs

Travel by land or ferry requires that you go through Canadian and U.S. Customs. The United States restricts most meats and all fresh fruits and vegetables from being brought into the country. The only meat allowed must be commercially canned. No freeze-dried meat is allowed, but other, meatless freeze-dried food is, along with other dry items such as bread and candy. For information on Canadian regulations, call their Excise and Taxation Information Service, 613-993-0534, and for the United States, 907-271-2686.

Lodging and Activities in Anchorage

Anchorage fills up during the summer, so make reservations well in advance. Bed-and-breakfasts, generally less expensive than hotels, are the preferable lodging option. Contact the Anchorage Chamber of Commerce for current information at 907-272-2401.

Climbers can purchase all their expedition food and equipment at the many large supermarkets and specialty food, sporting goods, and climbing stores.

The Anchorage Museum of History and Art, located near the corner of Seventh and A Streets, has an impressive number of displays on Alaskan history and indigenous cultures.

There are many nearby hiking and biking trails; information is available at the climbing stores.

Talkeetna
Elevation • 350 feet/107 meters

Most, if not all, expeditions planning to climb the West Buttress leave from Talkeetna, a colorful village with an adventurous past located 114 road miles/183 kilometers north of Anchorage and only 60 miles/97 kilometers from Denali. Situated on the confluence of three wild, silt-laden rivers, the Chulitna, Susitna, and Talkeetna, the village dates to 1916 when the search for gold became the stimulus for the construction of the Alaska Railroad. Originally named K'Dalkitnu—"River of Plenty"—by an Athabascan Indian band called the Mountain People, the village developed as a railroad construction work camp, but was sustained through the years by

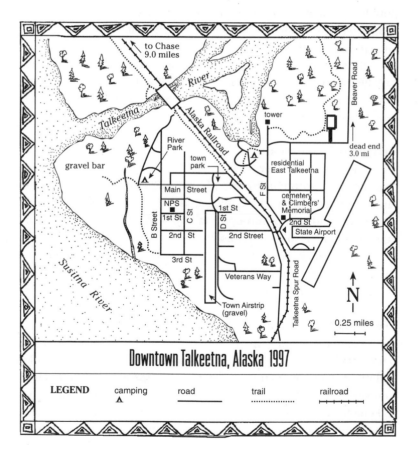

gold miners and prospectors who worked the gold-bearing grav-
els of the rugged Cache Creek mining district immediately west of
Talkeetna.

Fur traders, trading post operators, miners, and trappers lived
tough and colorful lives here, leaving behind log structures and a
historical legacy that has achieved recognition on the National Register of Historic Places. Constructed in 1923, the Fairview Inn now
hosts mountaineering groups from all over the world who gather
here to sing their homeland songs and celebrate their successes and
survivals in the great Alaska Range.

Today Talkeetna is a close-knit community of approximately 450
people that treasures its historical legacy and works continually to
maintain the qualities and natural resources that make it special. A
popular destination for outdoor enthusiasts, recreationalists, tour-
ists, fishermen, and photographers, Talkeetna embodies the essence
and spirit of Alaska.

There are few services in or near Talkeetna to outfit a climbing
expedition: a couple of small grocery and climbing stores, and a hardware store with an ATM money machine located 14 miles/23 kilometers outside of town.

Driving to Talkeetna

At Milepost Number 98.7 on the George Parks Highway, a side
road leads off to the north for 14.5 miles/23 kilometers and dead-
ends at Talkeetna. The drive takes about two-and-a-half hours from
Anchorage and passes through the city of Wasilla, where food and
equipment can also be purchased.

Most climbers sign up with a shuttle service based in Talkeetna
to transport them and all their gear to and from Anchorage. The cost
can vary, depending upon the number of people (see Appendix D).

Traveling by Train

Trains arrive daily in Talkeetna from late May to mid-Septem-
ber on their way to and from Anchorage and Fairbanks. Schedules
and prices increase as the tourist season approaches and it is best
to reserve at least a week in advance for tickets in June. There is a
$50 change or cancellation fee, which is almost the cost of a ticket.
The cheapest fare is the local Hurricane Special, leaving Anchorage

at 6:30 A.M. and arriving in Talkeetna at 9:30 A.M., running three times a week (see Appendix D).

Lodging and Activities in Talkeetna

Talkeetna boasts five inns, several bed-and-breakfasts and climber bunkhouses, and a campground. Contact the Talkeetna Chamber of Commerce for a listing, 907-733-2330.

Talkeetna is a truly unique and special community, rich with mountaineering and aviation history. During the summer, the casual, laid-back atmosphere in Talkeetna makes it ideal for passing the time walking around or watching a softball game. The town's museum has a grand relief model of Denali surrounded by large Washburn photos, exhibits that display early and modern climbing apparel, and a memorial to Ray "The Pirate" Genet, who created the first successful guiding company in Denali. Museum hours are 10:00 A.M. to 5:00 P.M.

A map of Talkeetna providing a self-guided historic walking tour through town may be obtained at the museum. If you continue to walk beyond the end of Main Street, you will arrive at the banks of the Talkeetna and Susitna Rivers where, in clear weather, you will be treated to a panoramic view of the Alaska Range. All climbers should pay a visit to the Talkeetna Climbers' Memorial, a beautiful but sad tribute to those who have lost their lives on Denali and the surrounding mountains. It is located in the cemetery next to the airport. Donations to help pay for new plaques and flowers are gratefully accepted by Diane Okonek on behalf of the Talkeetna Cemetery Association.

Registration

*I*n 1995, the National Park Service established a preregistration rule and registration fee. For the first time, mountaineers were required to pay to climb in Denali National Park and Preserve.

NPS regulations require all Denali or Mount Foraker expeditions *to preregister sixty days in advance of departure* and submit a nonrefundable, $25-per-person deposit toward a $150 registration fee. Only one additional member may join the expedition after that; he or she must preregister and send in a deposit within thirty days. Failure to do so within the specified time period denies access to the mountain. The NPS hopes the preregistration period will allow enough time to educate foreign climbers about the unique conditions encountered on Denali and Mount Foraker. The registration fee will help defray the cost of this effort.

Other mountains in the park outside the wilderness boundary, such as Mount Hunter and the Ruth Gorge area, require no registration. Presently there is much controversy about park regulations targeted at climbers and it is quite possible that the current rules will be reevaluated in the future. The NPS's reasoning is twofold: they wish to protect the safety of the inexperienced climber and prevent unnecessary rescues with their inherent risk and tremendous cost.

Denali and Mount Foraker climbers must also register at the NPS headquarters in Talkeetna before their departure. There they will submit their expedition itinerary, get briefed by rangers on safety and environmental concerns and proper waste disposal techniques, and pay the $125 balance of the registration fee. Upon returning, all registered climbers must also sign out.

The NPS does not have the authority to refuse anyone the opportunity to climb Denali as long as the individual preregisters and pays the fee. If the NPS staff assesses a climber as being unqualified or unprepared, they can only encourage the climber to get more experience before attempting Denali.

Contact the Talkeetna Ranger Station for a preregistration packet (see Appendix A). In order to avoid confusion, appoint one member of your expedition as correspondent to handle all communication with the NPS.

Equipment

*H*aving the right quantity of quality equipment can make all the difference on a Denali climb. The combination of extreme winter weather, high altitude, glacier travel, and expedition-style climbing tests gear to its limits. An efficient layering system will save time and hassle, and prevent exposure when protection is most needed. This said, *quality* does not necessarily mean *expensive*; a trip to the Army surplus store often turns up much of the basics. An Air Force nylon one-piece suit is considerably less expensive than a one-piece suit found in a climbing store.

The list below is not complete but rather suggests equipment that has worked satisfactorily during summer ascents of Denali's West Buttress.

Individual Gear

Traveling on a glacier poses the dilemma of having to dress for surface conditions—which in June and July are often extremely hot—while being ready for freezing temperatures in the event of a crevasse fall. Outside shell layers with ventilation zippers offer one solution. Another challenge in which clothing design plays an important role is how to "go to the bathroom" with ease and limited exposure. Half-moon zippers in the seat are one effective solution.

When choosing clothing, preventing frostbite is the climber's biggest concern; the most greatly affected body parts are toes, hands, and noses. While some weather conditions are so bad that no amount of clothing will provide adequate protection, many cases of frostbite are a direct result of inadequate or too-tight clothing. Each extremity poses the challenge of needing to be adequately protected from the environment while not restricted in terms of dexterity.

Foot Protection

Wear *plastic double boots* with thick insoles that fit slightly large in order to accommodate swelling feet at higher altitudes.

Bring enough sets—at least three—of your preferred combination of *socks* to rotate during the climb. Bring a clean extra set saved just for summit day.

Vapor barrier liner socks (VBLs) or plastic bags help keep your inner boots drier.

Extra-warm synthetic *booties* with thick, closed-cell foam insoles are nice for wearing around camp.

Regular *gaiters* are sufficient below 14,200 feet/4,300 meters. *Supergaiters* with the rands glued to the shell provide more insulation and prevent boot laces from icing up.

Above 14,200 feet, it is essential that feet be clad in insulated *overboots* which completely surround the boot. Neoprene models are the warmest, but can be troublesome for clip-on crampons. Nylon models lined with insulation are not as warm, but are more easily worn with clip-on crampons.

Hand Protection

Bring a couple of pairs of heavy-weight, polypropylene *gloves* and save a fresh pair for summit day.

Bring two pairs of shelled *mittens* in case one gets lost or damp. Preferable models combine a thick insert with a windproof shell that fits over a gloved hand. One of the pairs can be extra-large over-mitts that fit over the primary pair of mittens, providing increased insulation.

Head and Face Protection

In extreme conditions when the face must be completely covered, the challenge is to adequately breathe and not fog up your eyewear. For the lower Kahiltna, protection from sun and heat is a major concern.

Carry two pairs of *sunglasses*—in case of breakage or loss—of high quality, dark glass, with a noseguard. Side shields prevent glare, but increase fogging.

A *sun hat with visor* is essential protection from intense sun. Use a *bandanna* to protect your ears and neck.

In windy and cold conditions, double-lensed, dark *goggles* with air slots on the side will help protect your face.

There are many models of *face masks* to choose from, but none work all that well. Try an oversized pile or windproof *neck gaiter* that can be pulled up over your nose.

Body Protection

Invest in a large, expedition-quality *parka* with a firmly attached hood and inside water bottle pockets. Your parka should be easily accessible at the top of your pack.

Insulated *overpants,* down or synthetic, should have full side zippers and be large enough to wear over all your other layers. This layer substitutes for pile pants, which are a world of hassle to put on and take off under shelled pants and a harness.

Sleeping Gear

A warm night's sleep is a basic requirement to endure an ascent of Denali. *Sleeping bags* should have 4–5 pounds/2–2.25 kilograms of quality down or 5–6 pounds/2–3 kilograms of synthetic fill. A three-season bag with an insulated overbag will also work. The sleeping bag should be cut large enough to accommodate water bottles and inner boots while wearing most of your layers.

Two full-length *ground pads,* with a combined thickness of 1 inch/ 2.5 centimeters, are adequate for sleeping upon. Inflatable Thermarests are particularly good insulation from the snow.

Miscellaneous Personal Items

An *altimeter* is useful for navigating in a whiteout on the lower glacier and for monitoring air pressure.

Ear plugs aid a good night's sleep in a storm or when your tent partner is snoring.

A one-quart water bottle—clearly marked!—makes a good *pee bottle,* saving a trip to the toilet during the night.

Pee funnels for women, used in conjunction with a pee bottle, exist in various models; it is best to practice with them at home first.

A one-quart *thermos* stores extra hot water and can be a life-saver on summit day.

Wide-mouthed *water bottles* are easier to fill with a ladle.

Group Gear

Camping Apparatus

A small *FM radio* with antennae is able to pick up music stations from Anchorage. This helps pass the time while waiting out a storm.

Four-season dome-style *tents* with large cooking vestibules work well. The fly should have numerous reinforced tie downs, preferably midway up as opposed to around the bottom edge. Small stuff sacks attached to the ends of guy lines can be filled with snow and buried a foot down to make effective tent anchors. Guy lines are easily adjusted with small, three-holed plastic sliders, available at camping stores.

When it comes to *snow saws,* it is worth being a connoisseur. Look for a lightweight saw with alternating flared teeth, a stiff, sharp nose, and a large, angled handle. The Japanese saws imported by the climbing stores in Anchorage and Wasilla are most effective. Keyhole saws found at most hardware stores also function well.

Carry at least two snow shovels per tent. Shovels take a beating on Denali; be sure not to pry out blocks or they will crimp. Carry a steel garden spade for the bulletproof snow encountered above 11,000 feet/3,400 meters. Rectangular, flat blades work best with blocks.

Kitchen Apparatus

Given the time spent cooking and melting snow for water, thinking through your kitchen equipment list and strategy ahead of time will be well worth the effort.

White-gas stoves work the best in the cold and high altitude, and white gas is the most plentiful fuel on the mountain in case you run out. Self-cleaning models with shaker jets are the most reliable. MSR's XGK stove ranks well for heat output. Make sure the pot sits 1.5–2 inches/4–5 centimeters above the flame to reduce flare-up at high camp.

A *stove board,* which is essential for cooking on snow, can be as simple as a thin, rectangular piece of plywood. Pot boards are also nice for insulation and preventing snow from sticking to the bottoms of the pots.

Large-volume aluminum *pots,* four- and six-quart sizes for a three-person group, increase snow melting efficiency.

Small, plastic *cups* make effective ladles for soup and dippers for water.

Traveling Equipment

The decision to use *skis* should be based on all expedition members' skiing ability. Even the best skiers are challenged when it comes to skiing, roped, downhill, all the while trying to maintain the proper rope tension while carrying a backpack and pulling a sled.

When wearing *snowshoes,* safety tethers should be tied around the ankles to prevent losing the shoes in a crevasse fall.

Specifically designed 10-foot/300-centimeter *probe poles* (Ortovox) work best. Each rope team leader should carry one to speed up probing camp perimeters. Regular ski poles, with self-arrest grips and attached baskets, work well on the trail.

A *sled* is a crucial piece of equipment that allows the West Buttress climber to pull an extra 30–50 pounds/13.5–22.5 kilograms starting from base camp. Most popular are the lightweight, plastic "kiddy" sleds which need to be rigged and reinforced before they are glacier-worthy. Most air services provide the sleds, but bring plenty of six-millimeter perlon rope and utility cord for rigging.

Wands are used to mark caches, camp perimeters, the route, and summit day. Bring along sixty to seventy 4-foot/1.5-meters thin bamboo garden stakes with a square of colored duct tape attached to one end of each. Mark the tape with an identifying signature. Be sure to bring them all back down during descent.

Technical Equipment

A long ice ax, 60–70 centimeters, is more convenient to use on the moderately angled terrain of the West Buttress. Attach a tether from the ax head to your harness just long enough to allow for an overhead pick placement. This will prevent loss of the ax as well as allow for a quick change of hands when traversing a slope.

The technical climbing gear you choose for the climb should reflect a well thought out and practiced *glacier travel setup* for the number of climbers and rope teams on your expedition.

Mechanical *ascenders* should be easy to use, effective on an icy rope, and able to accommodate a mittened hand.

User-friendly *seat-harness* models allow the wearer to drop the leg loops while being tied to the rope in order to "go to the bathroom."

Chest harnesses are effective for keeping the climber upright during a crevasse fall.

Each climber needs to carry one or two *snow pickets,* or more, depending on the size of the team. Three *ice screws* are usually sufficient for the West Buttress during unusually icy conditions.

Repair Kit

A complete *repair kit* is a basic necessity on the West Buttress. All equipment is suspect to fail; you want to be prepared to strip clean a stove, splint a tent pole, or sew up a tent fly. Useful items include: nuts, bolts, washers, and screws; baling wire; hose clamps; snowshoe eyelets; utility string; ski binding material; ripstop nylon patch material; stove parts, including rubber O–rings and leather pump cups; cleaning needles; heavy and light sewing thread and needles; an entire extra tent pole; a pack belt buckle; heavy repair tape; an all-purpose Leatherman tool; and scissors.

Communication Equipment

A *two-way radio* has proven invaluable in emergencies and is useful for receiving the daily base camp weather reports as well as communicating with other parties. Citizens band, or CB, is the most commonly used frequency band, and channel 19 (27.185 MHz) the most common frequency, monitored by NPS, Kahiltna Base, and the air services. You do not need a license to operate a CB; however, a protocol exists for proper usage, including no use of profanity and keeping the conversation pertinent. Here is an example: "Mary Lou, this is Jim Bob, do you copy?" CB etiquette on Denali calls for switching to another channel for long transmissions.

You can either rent CBs from the air services or buy them at electronics stores in Anchorage and Wasilla. The most effective models have five watts, a long, telescoping antenna, and a removable battery pack. *Batteries* should be warm before using; it is wise to leave from base camp at 14,200 feet/4,300 meters with a fresh set. Condensation and trauma are the biggest problems with any electronic device so be sure to protect the radio when not in use. Check that your radio works while still in Talkeetna by calling an air service on channel 19.

CBs are line of sight and encounter transmission problems due to obstructions. If you receive no reply, assume the radio is working and broadcast your message in the blind. If an aircraft circles your camp and revs its engines, turn your radio on because the pilot wants to communicate with you.

Other types of transmitters work effectively on Denali, but are incompatible with most other parties on the mountain. Cellular phone service is available for the area and appears to work fairly well from Windy Corner up.

Medical Kits

Three weeks is a long time to be in a stressful environment. Every expedition should anticipate medical problems ranging from soft tissue injuries to gastrointestinal disturbances. *Medical kits* should include various-sized bandages, gauze, cloth tape, a thermometer, scissors, tweezers, antibacterial cleansers, and antiseptic cream. *Drug kits* should include medications to treat headaches, nausea, vomiting, constipation, diarrhea, indigestion, sore throat, infection, pain, inflammation, altitude-related illnesses, and tooth problems.

Rental Equipment

The climbing stores in Anchorage and the guiding companies in Talkeetna rent equipment (see Appendix E). Most of the air services also rent snowshoes.

Food

Nutritious and appetizing rations in the correct quantities with short cooking times require careful thought and planning and should involve input from all expedition members. It is a good idea to test the menus beforehand for quantity. Rations should reflect the abrupt change in conditions encountered above the 14,200-foot Basin Camp. Under 14,200 feet/4,300 meters, altitude plays a minor role in digestion, and pulling a sled allows you to carry bulkier items such as frying pans and bagels. Above that altitude, the lack of oxygen inhibits digestion, of fats in particular, so your diet should be higher in protein. Cheese and meats usually freeze solid. Everything is on your back, so lighter, more compact, one-pot meals are preferable.

Consider packing food in marked bags to make caching specific days of food easier. For larger expeditions, it is convenient to further divide each meal into tent groups so that in a storm, each group can grab their portions and retire to the shelter of their tents. This system requires that the kitchen also be divisible. A useful resource for planning rations is the *NOLS (National Outdoor Leadership School) Cookery* (see Appendix A).

Most food can be purchased in Anchorage at the many supermarkets, foreign specialty food stores, and wholesale membership food warehouses. There are also supermarkets in Wasilla. Talkeetna has limited supplies. You can usually arrange with the van shuttle services to stop by stores for an added fee per hour. Be sure to pick up a magazine and some fruit for the base camp manager!

Fuel

White gas (Coleman fuel) is by far the fuel of choice on the West Buttress. One cup of white gas per person per day is adequate with efficient cooking techniques (sixteen cups equals one U.S. gallon). It is necessary to purchase all your white gas from the air services and pick it up at Kahiltna Base where it is transported in bulk early in the spring. Federal aviation regulations prohibit transporting passengers and fuel on the same flight. Special arrangements must be made with the air service for climbers using butane or other fuels. Other forms of fuel are available at the climbing stores in Anchorage, Wasilla, and Talkeetna.

Climbing Strategy

Rope Teams

*T*he risk of falling into a hidden crevasse becomes reality from the moment the plane lands on the glacier. The most effective means of traveling safely on a glacier is to tie into one of two properly equipped and competent three-person rope teams. Single rope teams, especially with two members, accept greater risk as they are seriously limited in what they can do in the event of a crevasse fall. Solo climbers, regardless of their levels of experience and caution, are playing Russian roulette. Without X-ray vision, no one can determine the location or strength of all the snow bridges that must be crossed. Various contraptions comprised of ladders and poles have been used and do provide a degree of protection, but nothing is as effective as being on a rope team.

Glacier Travel Techniques

It is recommended that all expeditions spend a day practicing rescue scenarios at the crevasses north of Kahiltna Base.

Glacier Rigs

The many different types of glacier rigs that exist are well documented in the texts listed in Appendix A. Whatever setup you adopt, it is wise to practice and test it against the various crevasse fall scenarios that might take place: the middle or end person falls in; the victim is conscious or unconscious; the pack and sled must be retrieved; the victim must be hauled; and so on. There is no perfect glacier rig for every scenario, thus a certain amount of creativity is required for any real-life situation. Require that each member bring at least enough equipment to ascend a fixed line, build a snow anchor, and transfer a loaded rope onto it.

Expedition-style Climbing

Expedition-style strategies of one form or another are used to the exclusion of almost all other climbing strategies on the West Buttress. Expedition-style strategies involve shuttling supplies up the mountain, or "caching," as a way of reducing pack weight and allowing extra time for acclimatizing. The first carry brings a load of food, fuel, and extra equipment to the next camp location. The second move brings tents, kitchen, and personal gear. In essence, each member of the party climbs much of the mountain twice. When caching supplies, be sure to leave at least three days' worth of food and fuel back in camp in case a storm moves in, or some other unexpected reason causes a delay in reaching your supplies.

Probing while Traveling

While it is important to know the existence of any crevasses within a camp perimeter, this information is not vital while on the trail. The concern en route, partly in the interest of speed, is if the snow bridges spanning the hidden crevasses are strong enough to carry body weight. This can be fairly well determined by probing with a regular ski pole with a basket attached. The basket displaces more snow, better simulating a footstep. Ski poles also aid your balance while spanning crevasses.

Self-arrest

Being able to self-arrest using an ice ax is a fundamental mountaineering skill, essential for climbing on the steeper snow slopes above the 11,000-foot/3,400 meter Motorcycle Hill Camp. Preventing a crevasse fall on the moderate terrain found below 11,000 feet can usually be accomplished with good body position and proper rope tension, thus allowing the use of two ski poles, one with a self-arrest grip, while the ice ax is secured to the pack.

Running Belays

Placing running protection, such as snow pickets, to anchor the rope while climbing roped together on exposed terrain is a belay technique used frequently going around Windy Corner, on the 16,200–17,200-foot/4,900–5,200-meter ridge, and while traversing Denali Pass. The middle people on the rope team are advised to rehearse techniques for clipping through the running protection (wearing mittens). Yelling "Anchor!" when passing or removing running protection helps the leader know when to place another piece.

Fixed Lines

The steepest section of the West Buttress route involves 800 feet/ 240 meters of 45-to-55-degree ice, usually protected by two parallel sets of fixed rope. The fixed lines are notorious for traffic jams caused by climbers failing to pass anchor points efficiently, ascending the descent line, flipping over backwards with heavy packs, or having their crampons fall off. It is wise to practice on a simulated slope beforehand.

No one is officially responsible for the quality and care of the fixed lines or the pieces of protection anchoring the fixed lines to the slope. By default, some of the guiding companies have taken it upon themselves to replace the fixed lines when necessary. Lead climbers should check the anchors for adequacy while ascending the fixed lines. They should also back up the fixed lines by clipping their rope to the anchors, effectively creating a running belay.

Wanding

The use of wands on the West Buttress is essential to mark caches, camp perimeters, route, and crevasses. Bring at least sixty thin, 4-foot-long bamboo garden stakes marked with colored tape and a unique signature. Get in the habit of wanding your route on every carry and whenever you know you will be retracing your path shortly, even in good weather, in order to insure safe passage, should conditions worsen. Summit day, the most important day for a well-wanded route, requires forty or more wands. The lead person places the wands every 1–1.5 rope lengths, which should allow for adequate spacing. On traverses, place the wands above the trail to prevent them from being knocked over by the rope and sleds. While descending, be sure not to knock over another party's wands with the sled or rope as that might jeopardize their safety. Be sure to retrieve all your wands when retracing your steps or they will become trash.

Traveling in a Storm

Whether planned or unplanned, you are likely to travel in poor conditions at some point during an ascent of Denali. Below Motorcycle Hill Camp, navigating in a whiteout is usually the biggest challenge, while above that altitude, winds and low temperatures carry the risk of frostbite or hypothermia. Cautious climbers temper their traveling strategies by including worst-case scenarios, such as possible crevasse falls, in their decision-making process.

A rule of thumb when planning to make a carry and the weather looks dubious is to "stick your nose into it" and evaluate the conditions firsthand. Wand the route well and be prepared to stop and cache supplies early, should conditions worsen. When planning to move camp and conditions are poor, leave the tents up until the last minute before making the final decision. It is better to feel confident about the move than to retreat in a worsening storm, only to find that another party has moved into your camp.

Traveling in a whiteout on a flat glacier can be a scary and surreal experience; imagine being inside a Ping-Pong ball. Without the guidance of your own preplaced wands, it is easy to become disoriented, stray off route, and innocently expose yourselves to hanging glaciers. You risk the same dangers following someone else's wands. Faced with whiteout conditions on unfamiliar terrain, the prudent decision is to wait for better visibility. It is possible to travel from 7,900 feet to 10,000 feet on a compass bearing 10° east of magnetic north.

Preparing the Sled

Most West Buttress climbers haul their gear in sleds to the 14,200-foot Basin Camp. A convenient way to pack the sled employs a lightweight, large nylon duffel bag or stuff sack. All items are stored in the duffel which is tied securely to the sled to prevent loss of equipment in the event of a crevasse fall. The sled should be attached to the climbing rope using a prussic knot off the rear with a separate piece of small-diameter perlon cord to prevent it from slamming into the climber to whom it is attached. Divide equipment evenly among everyone to avoid loss of all of one item—for example, all the pots—should the sled be unrecoverable. Keep the weight low and toward the rear to prevent the front of the sled from nosediving in and flipping over. The sled bag should be tightly strung, but not so tight that the sled begins to torque out of shape. Avoid unnecessary trail breaking by tucking the sides of the duffel into the sled. From Kahiltna Base to Motorcycle Hill, the ratio of sled to pack weight should be around 60/40; on the steeper terrain above Motorcycle Hill, the ratio should be reversed.

Trail Etiquette

When two expeditions traveling in opposite directions meet on the same trail, proper etiquette calls for the descending party to give right-of-way to the ascending party. Below the Headwall and on Motorcycle Hill, descending parties should break a separate trail to avoid destroying the steps for uphill traffic.

Camping Techniques

*Y*ou camp up Denali, you don't climb it." This is a common remark heard among West Buttress veterans and reflects the effective climbing strategy of pushing from camp to camp, inching your way up the mountain. Probing out perimeters, building walls, maintaining camps during storms, staying extra nights to acclimatize, and moving short distances all contribute to more time spent camping than climbing. The most valuable quality to possess on the West Buttress is being a strong winter camper.

Choosing a Site
The photos in this guide indicate the most popular camps on the route. These sites have been chosen for their natural protection against wind, crevasses, and avalanches, and their proximity to each other in terms of altitude and distance. These camps also tend to be the most populated. Many other suitable camp locations exist. Those who prefer solitude should plan their camps away from the ones marked.

It is not uncommon to be so pinned down by the weather while moving camp that you are not able to move either upward or retreat back. Be prepared to camp almost anywhere in an emergency. Be on guard for exposure to serac fall and slab avalanches, and try to pick a location that appears crevasse free.

Probing for Camp
All camps should be probed, and their perimeters marked. Probing a site can be accomplished quickly and effectively or slowly and incompletely. Probing the snow with a specially designed probe pole (Ortovox) is the most effective means for determining where crevasses are hidden. When approaching the site, the rope team should move until the leader is at the far perimeter. At this point, the leader will be able probe back and forth, belayed by the second person, while the rest of the team is stationary. First probe an area just big enough to bring everyone into. Then probe for tents, kitchen, and latrine. The probed zone should be marked well with wands. Everyone's motto should be, "Step out of the probed area for a photo, fly home in a body bag." More than one climber has performed this exact act on Denali.

Shelters
A number of different snow shelters can be used on the West Buttress: igloos, trenches, and caves. Responsible climbers must know how to build these structures in the event that conditions are so extreme that a tent is lost or destroyed. Good-quality, four-season tents, however, are still the most practical and comfortable shelters in most situations. With adequately built snow walls offering protection from the wind, tents are the warmest types of shelter, taking advantage of the greenhouse effect provided by long days and

increased ultraviolet radiation. Under the right conditions, tents can also be pitched in bergschrunds.

Extreme weather situations and/or steeply angled slopes with no available bergschrunds warrant the use of snow caves. Igloos are the most comfortable snow shelters and are particularly effective on the flat terrain encountered at 17,200 feet/5,200 meters. However, Denali is not the place to learn how to build an igloo you will need to rely on. To build one quickly and well requires a high degree of skill and practice.

Walls

Tents require thick snow walls for protection against the wind. Denali camping etiquette declares all empty campsites open to anyone; at popular locations, vacated walled camps are often available. Walk around and check out the real estate. Even a camp with weak walls may be rejuvenated with enough chinking, and will save you the time and effort required for starting afresh. Sharing a common wall with another expedition also saves time and effort, but ask first.

Fortified camp notched into the ridge at 16,200 feet.
©Brian Okonek

Extra thick walls at High Camp ensure a good night's rest.
©*Brian Okonek*

With too many people sharing walls it becomes difficult to shovel out your site without throwing snow on someone else's.

When building a new wall, make sure that the tent area is paced out carefully and the boundaries marked. Start by digging down one foot for the entire tent area, and then use that snow for the walls. When building during a storm, begin with the windward wall in an effort to gain some immediate protection from the elements. How hard the snow is will determine whether to use shovels or saws to cut blocks. Effective walls rise above the ground surface and deflect the wind. "Bomb shelter" pits dug straight down into the snow fill in rapidly with drifts. Walls should be 15–30 inches thick, as high as the tents, and fully enclosed with the entrance facing away from the prevailing wind. Enough space should exist between the wall and the tent to allow for walking and careful shoveling during a storm.

A quarry is necessary in order to make snow blocks. A suitable site has snow with a consistency of styrofoam that produces strong, compact blocks. Avoid trampled snow, which produces weaker blocks. Above 11,000 feet/3,400 meters, the snow can be rock hard with hidden ice layers that bind up the saw. Probe in search of a drift of softer snow from which to saw blocks. Traditionally, Native Alaskans determined the location of their camps on the basis of proper snow density.

Setting Up the Tent

The most vulnerable time for a tent is during its pitching. Dome tents, especially, make great kites when not anchored down. Every year, unlucky or careless climbers watch the eerie spectacle of their tents disappearing into the clouds, along with their summit dreams. Designate one person as "tent holder," the one who does not release a firm grip until at least three anchors are set.

In a tent with two entrances, the larger vestibule, when pointed into the snow wall, can be used as the kitchen during a storm.

Tent Maintenance

When more than one-third of a tent is buried, it is in risk of collapsing. When digging out the tent, take care not to rip the fly. Use a mittened hand instead of a shovel blade to brush away the snow.

Moisture from breathing can cause significant hoar frost buildup overnight on the inside tent walls. Sweep it up with a mini-whisk broom and pot lid to prevent sleeping bags from getting damp.

Kitchen and Cooking

Outdoor kitchens can be as creative as you have time for building, but the usual is a walled pit with a high cooking counter and low seating benches. Most veteran guides use a pyramid/center pole–style fly to shelter the kitchen. Keep a sledful of clean snow for melting into water easily accessible. Dig a deep sump hole for wastewater. With freezing overnight temperatures, you'll want a nighttime "cabinet" in which to store enough water for breakfast. Wrapping the pots in a garbage bag first and then sealing the cabinet with snow will help insulate them.

Cooking in tent vestibules is a necessary luxury in order to stay warm and dry during a storm or when higher on the mountain, but requires prudence to avoid tent fires and carbon monoxide poisoning. First, the designated cook should be properly organized to avoid having to get up until after the meal. Have all the necessary snow cut into small, accessible blocks. Stoves should be full of fuel and all other cooking items and food for the meal should be accessible. The most dangerous part of cooking is priming the stove. Have a pot lid handy to shield high flames and be ready to toss the stove out the vestibule door if it flares up out of control.

Keep the kitchen tent area well ventilated; carbon monoxide is tasteless, odorless, and deadly.

Turning snow into water takes more time than any other kitchen chore. Increase your snow melting capacity by using a large pot (four to six quarts) and not allowing it to deplete less than half full before adding more snow. Be sure you have all your breakfast water ready and stored the night before.

Contaminated snow is a serious health problem at all popular camps. It is best to go to a far perimeter devoid of any human activity and fill sleds or plastic bags with clean snow to be hauled back to camp.

Human Waste and Garbage

Successful disposal of feces and garbage challenges mountaineering expeditions worldwide; Denali is no exception. The large numbers of people on the West Buttress generate tons of waste. Climbers used to throw all their waste into crevasses, but too many missed shots left garbage exposed for ravens to tear apart. This led to the formation of regulations prohibiting all but feces to be thrown in crevasses; everything else has to be carried off the mountain. This rule and the existence of latrines at the crowded camps at Kahiltna Base, Basin Camp, and High Camp have greatly reduced the visual impact of human waste on the mountain. The problem has not been eliminated, however, and at fault are the climbers who fail to find deep enough crevasses, or do not get close enough for an accurate throw, or find themselves on the trail needing to go but without a plastic bag. Burying feces in the snow leads to ugly melt-out later.

Plan on dumping the feces bag(s) as your last chore before leaving camp for good. Rope up and head for the closest deep crevasse.

Urine also has an offensive visual impact and is a source of contamination. Kahiltna Base, Basin Camp, and High Camp have designated pee holes next to the latrines, which greatly reduce the unsightliness of multiple pee holes dotted throughout the camps. Otherwise, be sure to designate one pee hole soon after establishing camp, thereby reducing the problem of finding clean snow for water.

Abandoned caches of surplus food, fuel, equipment, and wands is a growing trash problem. Leaving these caches is prohibited. If you cannot give your surplus away, you must haul it back to Kahiltna Base. Lighten this load by keeping garbage dry and compacted to reduce weight and bulk.

Three Ways to Build a Toilet

Plastic toilet seat method. Build a snow bench. Use a saw to cut out a slot in the middle for the trash bag. The width of the slot should be the same as the toilet seat hole. Round out the slot base for greater collection capacity. Place a large trash bag up through and around the toilet rim and tighten the fit with an overhand knot. Lay two snow pickets lengthwise along the snow bench and under the toilet seat for support.

Squat/trench method. Stomp out a 3-foot/1-meter square and dig out a 10-x-12-inch/25-x-30-centimeter by 2-feet-/0.6-meter-deep trench along its middle and line it with a garbage bag. Keep the bag in place with wands.

Ice ax method. Stand up two ice axes over which are draped the edges of a plastic bag. Sit lightly on the adzes!

Whatever the method, your latrine should be downwind of camp and protected by snow walls. Trying to go to the bathroom in a storm without wind protection, and snow filling up your pants, is a horrifying experience and leads to "holding it" and constipation. Make an effort to decrease bag weight by urinating beforehand. Place a block of snow over the opening to prevent snow from filling up the bag. Mark a sled for hauling feces bags; this sled should never be used for collecting snow for water. The same holds true for any shovel used near the latrine.

Caches

Many expeditions have failed on account of caches lost to heavy snowfall, wind, or ravens. Dig a snow hole large enough to bury all supplies 3 feet/1 meter under the surface. Mark the four corners of the hole with wands; tape three together for an extra-high center marker. The center wand should be driven deep enough into the snow to prevent it from melting out and falling over. To the center wand, tape a clear plastic bag in which there is a note stating your expedition's name and expected return date. Unmarked caches are considered abandoned by NPS patrols.

Ravens are of particular concern on a West Buttress climb. These industrious birds are always on the lookout for a meal and can dig up an amazing amount of snow to locate a cache. They also have been known to dig up locked duffel bags, peck little holes through the fabric, and pull out all the contents. The ensuing mess gets spread out all over the glacier by the wind.

Camp Etiquette

Once you move out of your camp it becomes available for others to move into. Burying a cache in the middle of your walled area as a way of saving your spot for the descent is considered poor style and frowned upon.

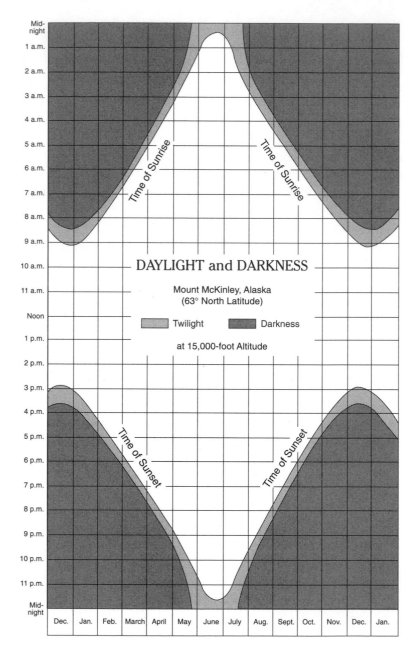

DAYLIGHT and DARKNESS

Mount McKinley, Alaska
(63° North Latitude)

Twilight   Darkness

at 15,000-foot Altitude

©Bradford Washburn

Approach,
•
Route,
•
Descent
•

THE APPROACH

To REACH THE BASE OF MOUNT McKINLEY, you can either hike for ten days or fly for thirty minutes. On rare occasions, expeditions seeking a full Alaska experience choose to walk, usually as part of the descent. But the majority of West Buttress climbers fly onto the Kahiltna Glacier.

Flying In

Historically, Alaska's bush pilots and their planes have shared a close relationship with Alaskan mountaineering. Ski-equipped planes, some requiring a minimal takeoff and landing distance, allow the mountaineer to bypass miles of mosquito-infested swamp and impenetrable bush. Flying into the Alaska Range in a small bush plane, squeezing through narrow passes and skirting 1,000 feet of sheer granite face is an unforgettable experience.

Although Washburn's 1951 expedition landed farther up the Kahiltna, current park regulations limit landing sites to outside the old park boundary. For the West Buttress climber, the closest place is 7,200 feet/2,200 meters on the southeast fork of the Kahiltna, known as Kahiltna Base. Planes are usually able to land there through the middle of July before snow and crevasses make conditions too hazardous. If you anticipate a mid- to late-July departure, you would be wise to include a contingency plan for hiking out (see "Descent" for hike-out options).

Many Talkeetna air services are prepared to fly expeditions onto the southeast fork of the Kahiltna Glacier. Their rates vary and they all offer a variety of incentives to fly with them: bunkhouses, fuel, wands, sleds, CBs, snowshoes, storage space, and personalized attention. Make reservations in advance to ensure that the air service will be ready for you. The most common plane used for landing on the southeast fork is the Cessna 185, capable of carrying three people and approximately 125 pounds/56 kilograms of gear per person. Plan

Approach

Central Alaska Range

on arriving in Talkeetna the day before your scheduled departure date and check in with your air service to determine the best time to fly. Often the weather is unflyable and expeditions have to wait in line for a clearing and their turn to fly. The "Talkeetna Hang" is another part of the whole experience. There are lots of ways to pass the time—see "Activities in Talkeetna"—but carry a CB when away from the airport in order to check in with your air service if you hear a plane taking off. Conditions change at a moment's notice and the windows of flyable weather do not always last long. It is advisable to be dressed for the glacier and have your equipment ready for loading.

Packing the Plane

Stuffing a bush plane full of expedition equipment, food, and climbers is a trick only the pilot is authorized to perform. Help expedite the job by having all gear organized into small piles next to the plane: ice axes, crampons, snow pickets, snowshoes or skis, ski poles, wands, shovels, sleeping pads, sleeping bags, and food bags. Inventory your gear to make sure everything makes it onto the plane. Should the weather prevent you from flying, "bombproof" your gear enough to survive the night; it can get windy at the airport.

Arriving at Kahiltna Base

After arriving and unpacking the plane, the pilot usually wants to take off immediately for fear of getting stranded in poor weather. Sometimes the plane needs help getting unstuck. Do exactly as the pilot requests and watch out for the propeller. Once your gear is unloaded, take care to secure any light items, such as sleeping pads, against being blown away by the propeller wind. As soon as possible, drag your gear off the runway to avoid any incoming aircraft.

Hiking In

There are a few possible routes for an approach onto the Kahiltna Glacier and none of them are easy. The closest road head is Cache Creek on the Petersville Road, 40 miles/64 kilometers (mostly unimproved) due west of Talkeetna. A common route is to descend Cache Creek and travel directly to the toe of the Kahiltna and up, 35 miles/56 kilometers to the southeast fork. The easiest way to travel is on skis, early in the spring. Most of the bears are hibernating, the rivers are frozen, and the famous Alaskan bush is buried under snow. Skiing is only possible, however, before spring breakup, when the rivers begin to melt and the snowpack begins to collapse—usually around mid-April. During the months of May and June, an overland approach is not feasible due to poor snow conditions. Later in the summer, staying high above the valley bottoms helps avoid the deep river crossings and the thicker bushwhacking. Be sure to practice proper bear camping and travel techniques to avoid hungry grizzlies. Allow for at least a week to approach Kahiltna Base from the road and be sure to discuss any route and check on current route conditions with the climbing rangers. See map, page 97.

Approach

THE ROUTE

ALL ELEVATIONS AND DISTANCES ARE APPROXIMATE. All names given to camps and locations are unofficial but generally have been accepted over the years.

Camp • **Kahiltna Base**
Elevation • **7,200 feet/2,200 meters**
Distance from Talkeetna • **60 miles/97 kilometers**
Elevation gain from Talkeetna • **6,850 feet/2,090 meters**

Located on the southeast fork of the Kahiltna Glacier, the views here are spectacular with the north face of Mount Hunter towering above, the east face of Mount Foraker dominating from across the Kahiltna Glacier, and the south face of Denali clearly visible through the saddle between Mount Frances and Peak 12,200 feet/3,700 meters. Kahiltna Base is typically a beehive of activity with climbers arriving, waiting to depart, and preparing for their climbs.

Camped on the southeast fork for the season is the Kahiltna Base Camp manager. The manager's primary responsibility is to provide information to the pilots about landing conditions on the southeast fork. Using a radio phone, the manager is able to update pilots in Talkeetna before they take off. Other responsibilities include maintaining a marked and packed runway which, after a snowstorm, requires all climbers' participation.

LEGEND FOR ROUTE PHOTOGRAPHS

———————	Route	▲	Camp
- - - - - - - - -	Alternate Route	■	Alternative Camp
———————→	Direction Arrow	X	Crevasse for Human Waste
- - - - - - - - ⇀	Avalanche Path		

(#3242) View up the Kahiltna Glacier. ©Bradford Washburn

South Buttress

#3242

Cassin

West
Rib

▲17,200'

16,200' ■

14,200 ▲

Windy Corner

KAHILTNA PEAKS

MT FRANCES

Southeast Fork

▲ 7,200'

Kahiltna Pass

Northeast Fork

East Fork

Kahiltna
Glacier

7,800' ▲

9,700' ■

N

Base camp managers have always been uniquely charitable, caring, and fun-loving individuals. They enjoy keeping track of expeditions' progress and provide weather reports over the CB at scheduled times. Their generosity is often misinterpreted by climbers who then treat them like "hosts." Take care to respect the manager's privacy. Ask permission to enter his or her shelter, and do so during business hours only. Offer your assistance, and do not ask to use the phone except in a real emergency. Upon arrival, introduce your expedition to the base camp manager and present the base camp card given to you by your air taxi. This document is proof of your gas purchase and registers your expedition with the base camp manager until your flight out.

Upon return to base camp after your climb, check in with the manager to schedule your flight out. Be prepared for the weather to have the final say concerning when you return to Talkeetna.

Hazards. Kahiltna Base is fairly protected from the weather, with winds rarely exceeding 30 miles/48 kilometers per hour.

Kahiltna Base is neither probed nor wanded, and over the years an occasional crevasse has opened up in the middle of camp. While roping up in the plane is obviously inconvenient, the fact remains that crevasses lurk everywhere. The casual ambiance at Kahiltna Base is misleading. Climbers are strongly advised to stay within the confines of camp, and probe with a keen eye.

An almost 7,000-foot/2,100-meter jump in elevation makes the flight from Talkeetna the biggest elevation gain of the climb. This increase is not life-threatening, but can cause mild AMS. Start good acclimatization habits early by consuming a quart of water upon your arrival. It is highly recommended that you spend at least one night at 7,200 feet/2,200 meters to order to acclimate before moving higher.

Human Waste. There are two pit latrines and adjacent pee holes in camp. Be sure to use them and don't create more pee holes in camp. Trash is forbidden in the latrines.

Notes. There is a good chance upon your return to Kahiltna Base that poor flying conditions will leave you stranded there for a few days. As a precautionary measure, leave a deeply buried and well-wanded four-day emergency food and fuel cache in the area behind the Base Camp manager's tent. Be sure that all food is sealed in waterproof containers or bags.

Immediately prior to landing, you will have a good view of crevasses just north of camp upon which to practice crevasse rescue.

Route Section • Kahiltna Base to Ski Hill
Travel • 7,200–7,800 feet/2,200–2,400 meters
Distance • 5.5 miles/9 kilometers
Elevation gain • 600 feet/180 meters

From Kahiltna Base the route descends Heartbreak Hill which, if icy, can be a frustrating experience for skiers unfamiliar with roped travel. The route swings wide where the southeast fork meets the main Kahiltna, in order to avoid the crevasse field along the south side of Mount Frances. Not far past the junction, you can choose between a direct route through the crevasse field immediately west of Mount Frances or swing farther west, staying on the smoother center of glacier flow. The route follows the center of the flow to the base of Ski Hill.

Traveling north, you will pass the east fork of the Kahiltna, which provides access to the South Buttress and south face of Denali, east of the Cassin. On the opposite, or west, side of the Kahiltna is Mount Crosson, which at 12,800 feet/3,900 meters is the seventh highest mountain in the Alaska Range. Separating the east and northeast forks of the Kahiltna are the beautiful and seldom-climbed Kahiltna Peaks. Ski Hill Camp, at the upper confluence of the northeast fork of the Kahiltna, provides access to the West Rib and Cassin Ridge.

Hazards. The lower Kahiltna acts like a reflector oven and should be avoided during the hottest parts of the day, especially in June and July. Plan on arriving in camp by 10:30 A.M.

This section has the largest crevasses and snow bridges on the entire route, another reason to travel at night when snow is firmer.

Notes. Sleeping during the day at Kahiltna Base in an attempt to switch over to a night schedule is difficult because of the noise from all the planes landing and taking off. Remember your earplugs.

Route

Camp • **Base of Ski Hill**
Elevation • **7,800 feet/2,400 meters**

Camp near the very base of Ski Hill as it is in a glacial compression zone and less prone to crevassing.

Hazards. With only a 600-foot/180-meter elevation gain there is little chance of altitude-related problems. Health concerns are primarily sun- and heat-related: dehydration, snow blindness, sunburn, and heat exhaustion.

This is the only camp other than the one at 7,200 feet/2,200 meters where the weather is usually forgiving and half-height snow walls are normally sufficient.

Waste Disposal. Not far down the glacier from the base of Ski Hill are numerous crevasses in which to deposit waste. You can also travel into the northeast fork. Carry any garbage to 11,000 feet/3,300 meters for caching.

Route Section • **Ski Hill to below Kahiltna Pass**
Travel • **7,800–9,700 feet/2,400–3,000 meters**
Distance • **2.5 miles/4 kilometers**
Elevation gain • **1,900 feet/580 meters**

Given the name for the frequently skied ramp between 7,900 and 8,900 feet/2,400 and 2,700 meters, the route follows the less-crevassed center, angling slightly north at the top toward Kahiltna Pass.

Most parties double-carry Ski Hill and wand it well for the return and second travel day.

Hazards. This section is also best climbed during the night to reduce heat fatigue and avoid soft snow. Weather systems and air masses out of the north and south funnel through Kahiltna Pass, so be prepared for poor weather. And because conditions gradually worsen as you gain elevation, you can expect to travel in a whiteout. It is easy to stray too far east (to the right) and expose yourself to serac fall.

Notes. In a whiteout, at an almost exact north-south bearing,

(#4912) Ski Hill. ©Bradford Washburn

use a compass for guidance. To help follow a bearing, use the first person on the rope as an extension of the magnetic north needle.

Camp • Upper Kahiltna Glacier
Elevation • 9,700 feet/3,000 meters

The upper Kahiltna Glacier is notorious for bad weather, which typically gets worse the closer you get to Kahiltna Pass.

Hazards. High winds call for fortified walls. Few crevasses are visible, but many exist. It is always important to probe thoroughly. Avoid exposure to ice falls along the east flank of the glacier.

Waste Disposal. Deposit waste in the crevasses found near camp or along the base of the ridge to the east.

Notes. In good weather and if time allows, climb the northeast ridge of Kahiltna Dome to acclimate and get one of the best views of McKinley and the lowlands. The ridge is heavily crevassed.

Route Section • Kahiltna Pass to Motorcycle Hill
Travel • 9,700–11,000 feet/3,000–3,400 meters
Distance • 1.5 miles/2.5 kilometers
Elevation gain • 1,300 feet/400 meters

The route rises gradually to 10,000 feet/3,050 meters before turning sharply east, contouring around a steep side hill. Past the corner, the route rises fairly steeply; one flat area is found at 10,800 feet/3,300 meters. The ascent turns abruptly north and into camp at 11,000 feet/3,400 meters.

Hazards. Take care not to stray within the debris zone of avalanches coming off the ridge to the north or south.

Notes. Most parties try to single-carry this short section. Another strategy is to double-carry to 11,000 feet and have half the team return for the rest of the gear while the other half builds camp.

Making the turn at the right place is nearly impossible in a whiteout without a properly wanded trail. Unfortunately, there are so many wands placed by lost parties groping their way through whiteouts

(#5033) 11,000-foot camp. ©Bradford Washburn

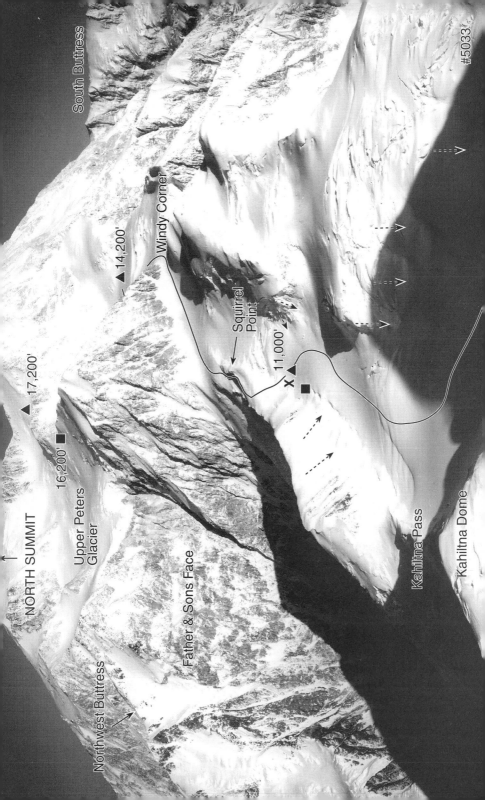

that the area has earned the nickname "Land of the Ghost Wands." Chances are good you will climb out of the bad weather once past the turn.

Camp: Motorcycle Hill
Elevation: 11,000 feet/3,400 meters

Situated in a small basin at the base of the steep Motorcycle Hill, 11,000 feet, is the staging location for surmounting the lower crux of the West Buttress, Windy Corner.

Hazards. The general vicinity of this camp is known for its many hidden crevasses. The camp itself fills up with expeditions, especially during periods of unsettled weather when Windy Corner prevents further progress upward. Climbers too often adopt a casual attitude, oblivious to the crevasse hazard, and walk around unroped to visit each others' camps.

Fatal cases of pulmonary edema have occurred at this camp; watch for signs from here on up.

Icefall hazard exists east of the camp basin. Look for fallen serac blocks within the camp perimeter, suggesting heightened glacier activity and good reason for camping farther west. However, the ridge west of Motorcycle Hill has been known to slab avalanche its entire length to Kahiltna Pass, so choose a protected location below a vertical rock band on the face.

Avoid becoming separated from your cached supplies because of a storm moving in. Leave at least a four or five day supply of food and fuel at camp when establishing a cache at Windy Corner.

Waste Disposal. The favorite locations for waste disposal are the crevasses northwest of camp. Seek out a deep crevasse, not a shallow depression, for the feces bag.

Notes. Remember to leave a cache of one day's worth of supplies for the return trip. Except when experiencing unusually deep snow, most climbers ascending from 11,000 feet switch to crampons and cache their snowshoes or skis. Huge amounts of snowfall here require exceptionally long markers.

Because of the topography, CB radios do not work well at 11,000 feet and above.

Route Section • **Around Windy Corner**
Travel • **11,000–13,500 feet/3,400–4,100 met**
Distance • **1.75 miles/3 kilometers**
Elevation gain • **2,500 feet/800 meters**

The route begins climbing straight up Motorcycle Hill, named after motorcycle competitions that attempt to surmount even steeper hills. From the small rocky knoll at the hill's apex is a spectacular view of the Northwest Buttress, Peters Glacier far below, and Peters Icefall above. The route heads west and traverses below, or to the north of, a rocky summit known for years as Squirrel Point, where, in 1993, sightings of a red squirrel surviving on abandoned food caches cemented the name. This section and the steep rise to the plateau before Windy Corner are exposed and can be icy, warranting the use of running belays. The plateau is a flat 0.5-mile/0.8-kilometer stretch traversing the base of the West Buttress to its right, or southern, corner, known as Windy Corner. As the name implies, wind velocities at this corner are severe, with frequent 60–100-mile-/100–160-kilometer-per-hour gusts. The few times the wind is not blowing might lure a climber into believing that the corner is a perfect camp location with its flat, panoramic view and numerous crevasse-free areas. The only protected camp nearby is in the buried bergschrund west of Windy Corner and north of Point 13,350 feet/4,070 meters. Turning the corner up closer to the buttress puts the climber in a better position to find the route through the coming crevasse field. The 13,500-foot/4,100-meter camp location will soon come up below and to the right.

Hazards. In stormy conditions, it is unwise to attempt to traverse Windy Corner, which has claimed at least three lives thus far. The plateau before the corner is heavily crevassed and the crevasse field on its eastern side is probably the most dangerous of the entire route. Many of the crevasses are perfectly hidden by a thin layer of windblown snow. Exposure while traversing the corner is tremendous. The slope is steep and icy, calling for running protection, especially with sleds, which tend to pull a person off balance. Rockfall and snow avalanches off the buttress are also of serious concern.

Notes. Most climbers feel the effects of altitude during this

Route

#3269

West Rib

14,200'

13,500'

Windy Corner 13,200'

Bergschrund

section of the climb and double-carry their loads. A good strategy is to cache around Windy Corner at 13,500 feet, and move camp all the way to 14,200 feet/4,300 meters and retrieve the cache the following day. The weather is less windy on the 14,200-foot side of the Corner, which increases your chances of being able to retrieve the cache should a storm move in.

Windy Corner cannot be seen from 11,000 feet/3,400 meters, but conditions there are nearly replicated at Squirrel Point, which is clearly visible. Long tails of snow blowing off Squirrel Point indicate the presence of high winds, which means that Windy Corner is probably impassable.

Because of the steeper and often icy terrain, you should pack your sleds lightly and use crampons and ice axes. Remove prussic knots from the rear of the sled in order to more easily pass any snow or ice running protection.

Camp • Around Windy Corner
Elevation • 13,500 feet/4,100 meters

The 13,500-foot camp is located 0.5 mile/0.8 kilometer east of Windy Corner, and is the first suitable camp located to the right, or south, between large, parallel crevasses. Your campsite needs to be chosen carefully here as there are many hazards to avoid.

Hazards. Huge crevasses abound! There are high risks of glacial advancement, collapsing bergschrunds, and snow avalanches off the buttress.

Waste Disposal. Choose the deepest crevasse on either side of camp.

Notes. This site at 13,500 feet is an alternative camp. For climbers suffering from the altitude, the move all the way to 14,200 feet/ 4,300 meters may wipe them out for the expedition; camping here is a wise decision.

(#3269) Windy Corner. ©Bradford Washburn

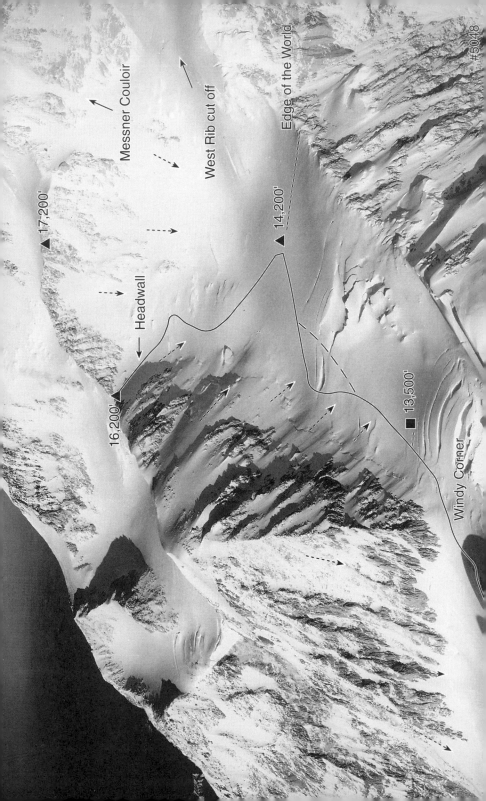

#5048

Messner Couloir

West Rib cut off

Edge of the World

17,200'

14,200'

Headwall

16,200'

13,500'

Windy Corner

Route Section • **Move to Basin Camp**
Travel • **13,500–14,200 feet/4,100–4,300 meters**
Distance • **1 mile/1.6 kilometers**
Elevation gain • **700 feet/210 meters**

A short, moderate climb flattens out into Basin Camp. A huge crevasse immediately before camp blocks the way and can be circumvented at its left, or northern, end, but usually there is a snow bridge offering a more direct route.

Hazards. Many climbers have been almost injured by rocks falling off the West Buttress. The route is exposed to the debris zone for avalanches off the buttress, and crevasses crisscross in abundance.

Camp • **Basin Camp**
Elevation • **14,200 feet/4,300 meters**

The large plateau at 14,200 feet serves as an advance base camp for West Buttress climbers as well as those waiting to climb other routes on Denali. Here the elevation and relative protection from weather allows climbers to acclimate while maintaining their strength. Higher on the mountain, climbers continue to acclimate, but the extreme environment tends to wear them down. It is advisable to spend at least four nights acclimating at this elevation.

The NPS maintains a camp here staffed with acclimatized climbing rangers available to assist in rescues and care for sick or injured climbers.

Hazards. Although it is not unusual to see climbers engage in a game of volleyball here, weather conditions can be extreme. Fifty-mile-/80-kilometer-per-hour winds accompany many of the storms; 3–5 feet/1–1.5 meters of snow falling in a twenty-four-hour period is not unusual. The temperature can drop to -20°F when the sun dips behind the West Buttress in the evening.

Crevasse hazard is historically nonexistent within the immediate confines of camp, hence the casual attitude and lack of wanded and probed perimeters. It is wise to probe camp, however, and as well the trail leading to the latrines and NPS camp.

(#5048) Basin Camp. ©Bradford Washburn

Most climbers commonly suffer from AMS during their first twenty-four hours at 14,200 feet, with symptoms that include headache, nausea, sleeplessness, and shortness of breath.

Huge avalanches have run off the West Buttress and Messner Couloir, almost wiping out the Basin Camp despite its long distance from the base of the slopes.

Waste Disposal. Due to the large number of climbers at this location, two pit latrines are maintained with adjoining pee holes. Be sure to use them and don't create more pee holes in camp. Trash is forbidden in the latrines.

Notes. A quarter mile south of camp marks the edge of the 14,200-foot plateau and a 4,700-foot/1,400-meter drop to the northeast fork. Known as the Edge of the World, this is a favorite excursion from camp for its magnificent views. Beware of the crevasses en route, particularly right before the Edge.

Plan on leaving a well-marked cache with sleds, food, and fuel for the descent.

In preparation for the upper mountain, clean and overhaul your stoves so that they burn more efficiently. Practice fixed-line ascending and descending techniques.

Route Section • Headwall
Travel • 14,200–16,200 feet/4,300–4,900 meters
Distance • 1 mile/1.6 kilometers
Elevation gain • 1000 feet/300 meters

Above 14,200 feet the real climbing begins. This section surmounts the West Buttress through a weakness in its southern flank and presents the steepest climbing along the entire route. A climb of 1,200 feet/370 meters of moderate terrain leads to an 800-foot/240-meter, 40-to-55-degree snow and ice face known as the Headwall.

Hazards. When a climber stops because a crampon has fallen off or an ascender has jammed, crowding on the fixed lines leads to major traffic jams. Efficient traveling skills while carrying a heavy pack on steep and icy terrain are essential.

Beware of icefall from the bergschrund while approaching the base of the fixed lines.

The entire Headwall has a history of slab avalanching and should be avoided after big storm events.

Crevasses between 14,300 and 15,500 feet/4,400 and 4,700 meters deep necessitate the use of standard glacier travel techniques.

Notes. Fixed lines protect approximately 800 feet of the Headwall and are unofficially maintained by the guiding companies, but their quality is not at all guaranteed. Two separate lines exist: the right, or east, for ascending, and the left, or west, for descending. The lines, which vary in thickness from 8 to 11 millimeters, are anchored with buried pickets about every 60 feet/18 meters. Treat the fixed lines as you would any climbing rope; inspect them for quality and take special care not to avoid piercing them with your crampons or ice axe.

Camp • Ridge Camp
Elevation • 16,200 feet/4,900 meters

Many climbers avoid this camp because of its exposure to wind and the difficulty of building a campsite on its steep and icy slopes. However, for those having trouble acclimatizing, camping at 16,200 feet breaks up an otherwise long move from 14,200 feet/4,300 meters to 17,200 feet/5,200 meters.

Chop out a level platform on the north face of the ridge and below the ridge crest for optimal wind protection. Build extra-thick walls around the north side of the tent platform. Digging a cave is also a good safety option for this location; at 16,200 feet, numerous tents have blown away or otherwise been demolished with their residents still inside.

Hazards. Strong winds and great exposure to steep and icy slopes have made this camp the scene of many epic survival stories. Consider fixing and clipping into a line while building camp, or to use as a hand line to get to your latrine. Anchor your tents and gear well. Under extreme conditions, tie the tents down with climbing rope clipped to anchors.

Be particularly careful not to slip or fall when walking around in overboots or booties without crampons. Always carry an ice ax.

Notes. Two snow caves are usually located below the ridge

Route

#6008

17,200'

Rescue
Gulley

Headwall

16,200'

X

crest, each capable of sleeping six climbers. Their entrances are usually drifted in with snow and discovered only after careful probing. The caves' perimeters are usually marked with wands to prevent people from collapsing their roofs. Their continued existence is a result of the extreme cold and annual maintenance by climbers. Do not count on their being available as they are popular.

Caches must be buried deeply here as strong winds can erode away the snow.

Route Section • 16 Ridge
Travel • 16,200–17,200 feet/4,900–5,200 meters
Distance • 0.75 mile/1 kilometer
Elevation gain • 1,000 feet/300 meters

This is perhaps the most interesting and spectacular section of the climb. The route follows below, or north of, the ridge line and weaves through the rocks. Several sections of steep and exposed climbing warrant the use of running protection. A short section below Washburns Thumb is usually equipped with a fixed line.

Hazards. The ridge line receives extreme winds from all directions and should not be attempted under stormy conditions. Winds from the south offer less cause for concern since the route follows the north side of the ridge. Many avoidable falls and frostbite cases have resulted from attempts to travel the ridge under poor conditions.

Camp • High Camp
Elevation • 17,200 feet/5,200 meters

High Camp is located on the barren, windswept plateau at the east end of the West Buttress, looking down on 14,200-foot/4,300-meter Basin Camp. The highest camp is also the windiest and coldest and demands the most fortification against the elements. Subsequently it is the most difficult and exhausting camp in which to build, and usually requires a rest day afterward.

Camps tend to cluster around the vicinity of the Rescue Gully.

(#6008) The spectacular ridge to High Camp.
©Bradford Washburn

Route

South Buttress

West Rib

Denali
Pass

17,200'

16,200'
X

#7215

This location is also near the experimental latrine and NPS rescue cache. Snow is usually quite hard and icy here, making it difficult to saw blocks. It is worth probing around in search of a windblown drift out of which to make a suitable quarry.

Most parties abandon their summit attempt within five days of waiting at 17,200 feet, usually due to the prolonged state of lethargy. It is essential to be physically active every day in order to maintain fitness. Wall-building "parties," natural history walks, or walking to dispose of the latrine box help to maintain fitness and acclimatization, and successfully help the climber through a long wait for summit day.

Hazards. Merely being at 17,200 feet is a hazard. The lack of oxygen (about half that found at sea level), extremely cold, dry air, and exposure to ferocious winds puts the climber at risk at all times. Be prepared for the worst.

Waste Disposal. Scattered feces is a big problem at 17,200 feet, due in part to the lack of nearby crevasses, but primarily to the climbers' failure to act responsibly under difficult conditions. Failing to build protected latrines, climbers defecate in the rocks along the edge of the plateau. These frozen "hockey pucks" become permanent additions to an otherwise beautiful setting until a conscientious person digs them up with a steel spade and disposes of them properly. In an attempt to solve this problem while unable to build pit latrines in the rock-hard snow, NPS has been experimenting since 1993 with a surface latrine that uses large cardboard boxes. This latrine has successfully concentrated human waste in one area, but relies on climber maintenance. When the box becomes three-quarters full, it should be hauled out of the latrine, placed on the sled, and taken to the nearest crevasse one-eighth of a mile northeast of camp. It is best to let the box freeze overnight and have four individuals help with the hauling in order to prevent capsizing. Built into the side of the latrine is a slot containing more cardboard boxes and large plastic bags. A new box is then assembled and lined on the inside and outside with plastic bags and placed in the latrine.

Like feces, pee holes remain year after year on the windswept

(#7215) The spine of the West Buttress. ©Bradford Washburn

Messner
Couloir

Rescue Gulley

Denali Pass
18,200'

17,200'

X

#7233

plateau. In order to decrease an already dire contaminated snow problem, climbers should use the existing pee holes near the latrine.

Notes. The NPS maintains a cache of rescue equipment at High Camp. This cache is usually equipped with a litter, oxygen bottles and regulator, a Gamow™ bag, and 1,000 feet/300 meters of static rope.

Summit Day • 17,200–20,320 feet/5,200–6,190 meters
Distance • 2.5 miles/4 kilometers
Elevation gain • 3,100 feet/900 meters

Summit day unquestionably stands out as the longest and hardest day on the mountain. The ascent can be broken down into thirds. The first and most notorious section ascends Denali Pass. The second part more or less follows the ridgeline along the southwest face to a large, flat plateau known as the Football Field. The final portion ascends the summit headwall and follows the summit ridge to the top.

Denali Pass can be reached with a long traverse from the southwest. Although it may not appear too steep or intimidating, the pass bears a long and frightful history of falls resulting in serious injuries and deaths. The traverse is in the shade until midmorning and extremely cold. It does receive late afternoon sun.

From the pass, head south up to the first group of large rocks to the east. An ongoing Japanese project to maintain weather-collecting instruments is located there—although it has blown down numerous times. Stay slightly to the left, east, side of the ridge, heading south until reaching the same elevation as Archdeacons Tower. Take a southeasterly course alongside a small ridge of rocks and over a small plateau, the back side of Archdeacons Tower. A short drop brings you to a 0.25-mile/0.4-kilometer plateau called the Football Field.

Once across the Football Field, ascend directly to Kahiltna Horn, gaining the summit ridge at 20,100 feet/6,100 meters. Kahiltna Horn is also the top of the Cassin Ridge. The 0.25-mile/0.4 kilometer, corniced Summit Ridge is the last obstacle to negotiate before reaching Denali's south summit.

(#7233) High Camp. ©Bradford Washburn

#4794

Talkeetna

Tokositna
Glacier

Football
Field

Archdeacons
Tower

Weather
Meter

Denali Pass

Harper Glacier

Summit Plateau, North Peak

Kahiltna Horn

Football Field

#7252

Archdeacons
Tower 19,650'

Weather Meter

Denali Pass

Weather
Meter

1947 Cosmic
Ray Camp

Denali Pass
18,200'

#57-543

Mt. Huntington

Kahiltna
Horn

South
Buttress

Pig
Hill

Football Field
19,500'

above: *Denali is not for everybody.* ©*Brian Okonek*
page 122: *(#4794) Traverse to Denali Pass.* ©*Bradford Washburn*
page 123: *(#57-5430) East side of Denali Pass.*
        ©*Bradford Washburn*
page 124: *(#7252) Ridgeline to the Football Field.*
        ©*Bradford Washburn*
page 125: *(#7250) Football Field.* ©*Bradford Washburn*
page 126: *(#7203) South summit and summit ridge.*
        ©*Bradford Washburn*

MT FORAKER
East Face

Kahiltna
Glacier

MT FRANCES

Southeast
Fork

East Fork

MT HUNTER

#57-5939

Hazards. Most accidents occur on the descent and usually fall within three categories: veering off route, getting pinned by weather, or falling while descending Denali Pass. The effects of altitude and cold, to a greater or lesser degree, contribute to all three categories.

The weather should be constantly monitored with a hasty retreat ready to be initiated if conditions deteriorate. Visibility can decrease to zero within minutes, and without a heavily wanded trail, it is easy to become disoriented and lost. Tragic stories about disoriented climbers walking off the southwest face and falling down the Messner Couloir, or heading off route while seeking shelter from a storm are unfortunately all too real.

One of the few predictable signs that the weather on Denali is turning for the worse is the formation of a lenticular cloud on top of Mount Foraker.

Long falls on Denali Pass are preventable using running protection and an ice ax instead of ski poles for self-arresting. Climbing guides typically bring twelve pickets to protect the traverse and leave them marked with wands for the descent.

Notes. The usual return time from the summit is eight to twelve hours. Being exposed for such a long time to everything Denali can hurl at you warrants bringing enough gear to survive another night out: all your layers of clothing; a stove, pot, and soup; two sleeping bags which zip together for every three people; a spade; and one or more saws. If you are caught out, it is worth searching for a snow drift to mole into or cut blocks from.

Be sure to wand your route well as visibility can drop to zero quickly.

Leave in place any carabiners, pickets, or ice screws you come across. Another expedition is probably depending on these anchors.

Stuff food into pockets for easy access and water bottles under layers of clothing to keep them from freezing. A thermos of hot water should be considered part of the medical kit.

Cameras should also be under layers to insure proper operation.

Pare down to the bare essentials. Bring a mini-first aid kit, including drugs for pain, HACE, and HAPE, and some gauze bandages—enough

(#57-5939) The view from the summit down the backbone of the Alaska Range. ©Bradford Washburn

to buy some time while the injured are brought back to camp. Bring a mini-repair kit that includes enough to mend a broken crampon: nuts, bolts, and wire.

Chemical hand and foot warmers or even battery-warmed socks are a great benefit on summit day.

In the event that a climber has to descend rapidly, the fastest route is down the Rescue Gully, using the 1,000 feet/300 meters of static line stored in the NPS's rescue cache.

THE DESCENT

WHILE IT IS FEASIBLE TO TRAVEL FROM High Camp to Kahiltna Base in one long push, breaking up the descent into two or three days is more humane and allows you to savor the experience, summit or no summit.

Weather conditions should still dictate the decision to move down the ridge to 16,200 feet/4,900 meters, and Windy Corner still presents a major challenge. But the incredible attraction of "smelling the barn" still leads to the occurrence of falls and frostbite when climbers try to push their descent during a storm. Patience is, as ever, the Alaska mountaineer's most valuable tool.

Packs are usually the heaviest during this stretch of descent unless you have completely exhausted your fuel and food supply. A heavy pack on a tired body moving downhill on exposed terrain is an accident waiting to happen. Remember: climb slowly, remain focused, and use running belays.

It is reasonable to descend from 17,200 feet/5,200 meters to 16,200 feet in a single push. Once you have arrived, rest and dig up any cache before tackling the fixed lines. One member of your party should look down the Headwall and check for crowds and windy conditions on the lines. Sometimes you will find climbers ascending the down line, which is poor etiquette but hard to rectify. Dress according to weather conditions before getting on the fixed lines.

Once at 14,200 feet/4,300 meters you will want to find your cache and make a decision to either push on to 11,000 feet/3,400 meters or camp. The condition of the individuals in your party and the weather are the primary factors to consider. If everyone is able and it is not too windy, the prudent decision is to keep going. Otherwise, it is quite possible to get stranded at 14,200 feet if Windy Corner becomes impassable.

With all this said, my most memorable descents involved spending the night at 14,200 feet, leaving at 10:00 P.M. the following day,

Descent

131

and traveling all the way to 7,200 feet/2,200 meters during the cool hours of the night. This allowed everyone to sleep in, have a feast brunch, hike over to the Edge of the World to pay our respects, and feel rejuvenated for the long haul to base.

Special circumstances need to be considered when roping up for the departure from 14,200 feet. This is usually the first time your expedition will be traveling downhill with loaded sleds. To keep the sleds from flipping, they need to be packed especially well; make sure they are not top-heavy. The last person on each rope team should not pull a sled. Instead, sandwich it, empty, with a teammate's. Team members pulling a sled will want the person behind them to maintain tension to prevent that sled from hitting the backs of their ankles. You will avoid much frustration if the sled prussic is adjusted perfectly and sled brakes (a knotted rope tied under the sled) are used.

Once you arrive at 11,000 feet, having passed the steepest terrain, consider having the climbers on the ends of the ropes retrieve their sleds. Upon reaching the bottom of Ski Hill (7,800 feet/2,400 meters), most people are ready for a long break, fresh socks, or even a short nap. The final push to Kahiltna Base allows for reflection because it takes so long, but hopefully the weather will allow for the spectacular view down the Kahiltna. Once at the base of the southeast fork, you will find out why Heartbreak Hill received its name, and once you see the latrine, you will know you are almost there.

Flying Out

Between 8:00 A.M. and 7:00 P.M., notify the base camp manager that your expedition has returned and you are requesting a flight out. Remember to pull your emergency food cache, consolidate all garbage, and organize your gear into piles as you did for the flight in.

It is often the case that plane service is backed up, most likely due to inclement weather. Do not be surprised to find yourself pacing the runway for days, eagerly listening for the drone of an approaching plane. Be prepared to leave gear behind to be put on a later flight. Consolidate it in a pile marked with your expedition name and ask the base camp manager for a designated spot near the runway.

Hiking Out

Expeditions wishing to hike out have the option of arranging to raft the Tokositna River, grade II, back to Talkeetna. A good route to the headwaters of the Tokositna descends 11 miles/18 kilometers of the Kahiltna Glacier to an unnamed fork on the east side at 4,400 feet/1,300 meters. Crevasses are numerous and bridges become increasingly unstable as you approach the firn zone, usually around 5,000 feet/1,500 meters. Take this fork 4 miles/6 kilometers up and over Second Shot Pass and 14 miles/23 kilometers down the Kanikula Glacier to the headwaters of the Tokositna River. Prearrange with your air service to drop off rafts at a gravel strip near the headwaters. Rafts, paddles, and life jackets can be rented in Talkeetna. This route should only be attempted by serious parties as it is an expedition in itself.

Sample Itinerary

Based on good conditions and good weather.

DAY 1 Arrive in Anchorage during the morning or previous night; purchase food and last minute items; drive to Talkeetna; check in with air service for departure time.

DAY 2 Dress for the glacier; register with NPS; organize gear at air service for the flight in; fill out a fuel card; fill water bottles; fly to Kahiltna Base; register with base camp manager; collect fuel.

DAY 3 Spend day practicing crevasse rescue techniques at nearby crevasses; go to bed early.

DAY 4 Leave camp by 3:00 A.M. (in June and July); single-carry to 7,800 feet/2,400 meters.

DAY 5 Carry to 9,700 feet/3,000 meters.

DAY 6 Move to 9,700 feet.

DAY 7 Single-carry to 11,000 feet/3,400 meters.

DAY 8 Rest day.

DAY 9 Carry to 13,500 feet/4,100 meters.

DAY 10 Move to 14,200 feet/4,300 meters.

Descent

DAY 11 Pick up cache at 13,500 feet.

DAY 12 Rest day.

DAY 13 Carry to 16,200 feet/4,900 meters.

DAY 14 Rest day.

DAY 15 Move to 17,200 feet/5,200 meters.

DAY 16 Rest day.

DAY 17 Summit day or pick up cache at 16,200 feet.

DAYS 18–21 Summit days.

DAY 22 Return to 14,200 feet or 11,000 feet.

DAY 23 Return to Kahiltna Base; check in with base camp manager for return flight.

DAY 24 Fly to Talkeetna; check out with NPS; visit the Climbers' Memorial.

DAY 25 Fly home.

APPENDIX A: Resources

Bibliography

American Alpine Club, "Accidents in North American Mountaineering," AAC Press, 113 E. 90th St., New York, NY 10128, 1977 to present.

Beckey, F., *Mount McKinley: The Icy Crown of North America.* The Mountaineers Books, 1001 S.W. Klickitat Way, Suite 201, Seattle, WA 98134, 1993.

Brease, P., and A. Till, "The Geology and Glacial History of Denali National Park and Vicinity," *Geologic Society of America Field Trip #9 Guidebook and Roadlog,* Cordillera Section Meeting, Fairbanks, AK, May, 1995.

Brown, W. E., *Denali, Symbol of the Alaska Wild.* The Donning Co./ Publishers, 184 Business Park Dr., Suite 106, Virginia Beach, VA 23462. Copyrighted with the Alaska Natural History Association, P.O. Box 230, Denali National Park, AK 99755, 1993.

Collier, M., *The Geology of Denali National Park.* Alaska Natural History Association, Box 230, Denali Park, AK 99755, 1989.

Davidson, A., *Minus 148°.* W.W. Norton & Co., Inc., New York, NY, 1969.

DuFresne, J., *Alaska—A Travel Survival Kit.* Lonely Planet, P.O. Box 617, Hawthorn, Vic 3122, Australia, 1994.

Fredston, J., and D. Fesler, *Snow Sense: A Guide to Evaluating Snow Avalanche Hazard.* Alaska Mountain Safety Center, 9140 Brewsters Drive, Anchorage, AK, 99516, 1994.

Graydon, Don, Ed., *Freedom of the Hills,* 6th ed. The Mountaineers Books, 1001 S.W. Klickitat Way, Suite 201, Seattle, WA 98134, 1996.

Hackett, P., *Mountain Sickness.* AAC Press, 113 E. 90th St., New York, NY 10128, 1980.

Herrero, S., *Bear Attacks, Their Causes and Avoidance.* Lyons and Burford, 1985.

Houston, C., M.D., *Going Higher.* Little, Brown & Co. Ltd., Boston and Toronto, 1987.

Mountaineering Rangers of Denali National Park and Preserve, "Mountaineering: Denali National Park & Preserve," Alaska Natural History Association, P.O. Box 588, Talkeetna, AK 99676.

Murie, A., *Birds of Mount McKinley.* Mount McKinley Natural History Association, 1963.

————, *Mammals of Denali.* Alaska Natural History Association, 1962.

Moore, T., *Mt. McKinley: The Pioneer Climbs.* The Mountaineers Books, 1001 S.W. Klickitat Way, Suite 201, Seattle, WA 98134, 1981.

Powers, P., *NOLS Wilderness Mountaineering.* Stackpole Books, 5067 Ritter Rd., Mechanicsburg, PA 17055, 1993.

Pratt, V. E. and F. G. Pratt, *Wildflowers of Denali National Park.* Alaskakrafts, Inc., 1993.

Randall, G., *Mount McKinley Climber's Handbook.* Chockstone Press, Inc., P.O. Box 3505, Evergreen, CO 80439, 1992.

Richard, S., D. Orr, and C. Lindholm, *NOLS Cookery.* Stackpole Books, P.O. Box 1831, Harrisburg, PA 17105, 1991.

Selters, A., *Glacier Travel and Crevasse Rescue.* The Mountaineers Books, 1001 S.W. Klickitat Way, Suite 201, Seattle, WA 98134, 1990.

Sherwonit, B., *To The Top Of Denali.* Alaska Northwest Books, 22026 20th Ave. S.E., Bothell, WA 98021, 1990.

Snyder, H., *Hall of the Mountain King.* Charles Scribner's Sons, New York, NY, 1973.

Stuck, H., *The Ascent of Denali.* Wolfe Publishing Co., Inc., 6471 Airpark Dr., Prescott, AZ 86301, 1988.

Tilton, B., and F. Hubbell, *Medicine for the Backcountry,* 2nd ed. ICS Books, Inc., 107 E. 89th Ave., Merrillville, IN 46410, 1995.

————, *The Basic Essentials of Avalanche Safety.* ICS Books, Inc., 107 E. 89th Ave., Merrillville, IN 46410, 1992.

Walker, T., *Denali Journal.* Stackpole Books, 1992.

Washburn, B., and D. Roberts, *Mount McKinley, Conquest of Denali.* Harry N. Abrams, Inc., New York, A Times Mirror Company, 1991.

————, "Mount McKinley from the North and West." American Alpine Club Journal, 710 10th St., Golden, CO 80401, pp. 282-293, 1947.

————, "Mount McKinley: The West Buttress." American Alpine Club Journal, 710 10th St., Golden, CO 80401, pp. 213-226, 1952.

Waterman, J., *High Alaska: A Historical Guide to Denali, Mount Foraker, and Mount Hunter.* AAC Press, 113 E. 90th St., New York, NY 10128-1589, 1988.

————, *Surviving Denali: A Study of Accidents on Mount McKinley: 1903-1990.* AAC Press, 113 E. 90th St. New York, NY 10128-1589, 1991.

Werner, A. "Glacial Geology of the McKinley River Area." MS thesis, Southern Illinois University, 1982.

Wilkerson, J., B. Cameron, and J. Hayward, *Hypothermia, Frostbite, and Other Cold Injuries.* The Mountaineers Books, 1001 S.W. Klickitat Way, Suite 201, Seattle, WA 98134, 1986.

Wilcox, J., *White Winds.* Hwong Publishing Company, Los Alamitos, CA, 1981.

Maps

The United States Geological Survey (USGS) provides standard topographical maps of Alaska. They can be purchased in Talkeetna or by request from the USGS, 907-786-7000.

"Mount McKinley, Alaska," 1:50,000, edited by Bradford Washburn. The best map available showing the West Buttress route on Denali. Suitable for framing. Available at climbing stores or by contacting Alaska and Polar Region Dept., University of Alaska, Fairbanks, Science Park, Fairbanks, AK USA 99775-1005; 907-474-6773.

"Denali National Park and Preserve," 1: 250,000.

"Talkeetna" D-3, and "Mount McKinley" A-3, 1:63,000. Shows the West Buttress.

"Talkeetna" C-3, C-2, B-3, and B-2, 1:63,000. Shows approach hike to the Kahiltna Glacier.

Bradford Washburn Photographs

Photographs can be obtained through the Boston Museum of Science and the University of Alaska, Fairbanks. Use the negative number of the print when ordering.

You can also contact Dr. Washburn directly at the Museum of Science, Science Park, Boston, MA 02114-1099; phone: 617-589-0228; fax: 617-589-0363.

In Alaska, contact Archives, Rasmuson Library, Alaska and Polar Regions Dept., P.O. Box 756808, University of Alaska, Fairbanks, AK 99775-1005; 907-474-6773.

DNP&P Mountaineering Rangers

Talkeetna Ranger Station, Denali National Park and Preserve, P.O. Box 588, Talkeetna, AK 99676; phone: 907-733-2231; fax: 907-733-1465.

APPENDIX B: Air Services

Doug Geeting Aviation
P.O. Box 4, Talkeetna, AK 99676
phone: 907-733-2366; fax: 907-733-1000; email: airtours@alaska.net

Hudson Air Service
P.O. Box 648, Talkeetna, AK 99676
phone: 907-733-2321; fax: 907-733-2333

K-2 Aviation
P.O. Box 545, Talkeetna, AK 99676
phone: 907-733-2291; fax: 907-733-1221; email: explore@alaska.net

McKinley Air Service
P.O. Box 544, Talkeetna, AK 99676
phone: 907-733-1765; fax: 907-733-1765

Spotted Dog Aviation
P.O. Box 786
Talkeetna, AK 99676
phone: 907-733-1800; e-mail: spotdog@arctic.net

Talkeetna Air Taxi
P.O. Box 73, Talkeetna, AK 99676
phone: 907-733-2218, 800-533-2219; fax: 907-733-1434; email:
flytat@alaska.net

APPENDIX C: Guide Services

The following companies, listed in alphabetical order, are authorized to guide on Denali. Contact the NPS in Talkeetna for the current listing.

Alaska-Denali Guiding, Inc.
P.O. Box 566, 2nd Street, Talkeetna, AK 99676
phone: 907-733-2649; fax: 907-733-1362; email: adg@alaska.net

American Alpine Institute
1515 12th St., Bellingham, WA 98825
phone: 360-671-1505; fax: 360-734-8890

Fantasy Ridge Alpinism
P.O. 1679, Telluride, CO 81435
phone/fax: 970-728-3546

Mountain Trip
P.O. Box 91161, Anchorage, AK 99509
phone: 907-345-6499; fax: 907-345-6499; email:
75523.3250@compuserve.com

National Outdoor Leadership School
288 Main Street, Lander, WY 82520
phone: 307-332-6973; fax: 307-332-1220; email:
admissions@nols.edu

Rainier Mountaineering, Inc.
535 Dock Street, Suite 209, Tacoma, WA 98402
phone: 206-627-6242; fax 206-627-1280

APPENDIX D: Transportation Addresses

Alaska Railroad
Pouch 7-2111, Anchorage, AK 99510
phone: 907-265-2685; 800-544-0552

Denali Overland Transportation
P.O. Box 330, Talkeetna, AK 99676
phone: 907-733-2384

Talkeetna Shuttle Service
P.O. Box 468, Talkeetna, AK 99676
phone: 907-733-1725, 888-288-6008; fax 907-733-2222

APPENDIX E: Equipment

Equipment Sales

Alaska Mountaineering and Hiking, Anchorage, 907-272-1811

Cellular World, Anchorage, 907-733-7177; rent cellular phones by
the week

Gary Kings Sporting Goods, 907-272-5401

Posh House, 907-248-6062

REI, Anchorage, 907-272-4565

Talkeetna Outdoor Center, 907-733-2230

Windy Corner, Talkeetna, 907-733-1600

Windy Corner, Wasilla, 907-373-6117

Equipment Rentals

Alaska-Denali Guiding, Inc., Talkeetna, 907-733-2649

Alaska Mountaineering and Hiking, Anchorage, 907-272-1811

Alaska Mountaineering School, Talkeetna, 907-733-1016

REI, Anchorage, 907-272-4565

Talkeetna Outdoor Center, 907-733-2230

Windy Corner, Talkeetna, 907-733-1600

APPENDIX F: Metric Conversions

To convert feet to meters, multiply by 0.3048.

To convert miles to kilometers, multiply by 1.609.

To convert °Fahrenheit to °Centigrade, subtract 32, multiply by 5, and divide by 9.

About the Author

Colby Coombs is a climber, Denali guide, and codirector of the Alaska Mountaineering School. Colby first reached the summit of Denali at age eighteen as Brian Okonek's client, and has been guiding and teaching mountaineering in the Alaska Range ever since. Notable climbs include the north face of Mount Hunter, the east face of Mount Foraker, and an alpine ascent of the Cassin Ridge on Denali.

THE MOUNTAINEERS, founded in 1906, is a nonprofit outdoor activity and conservation club, whose mission is "to explore, study, preserve, and enjoy the natural beauty of the outdoors. . . . " Based in Seattle, Washington, the club is now the third-largest such organization in the United States, with 15,000 members and five branches throughout Washington State.

The Mountaineers sponsors both classes and year-round outdoor activities in the Pacific Northwest, which include hiking, mountain climbing, ski-touring, snowshoeing, bicycling, camping, kayaking and canoeing, nature study, sailing, and adventure travel. The club's conservation division supports environmental causes through educational activities, sponsoring legislation, and presenting informational programs. All club activities are led by skilled, experienced volunteers, who are dedicated to promoting safe and responsible enjoyment and preservation of the outdoors.

If you would like to participate in these organized outdoor activities or the club's programs, consider a membership in The Mountaineers. For information and an application, write or call The Mountaineers, Club Headquarters, 300 Third Avenue West, Seattle, Washington 98119; (206) 284-6310.

The Mountaineers Books, an active, nonprofit publishing program of the club, produces guidebooks, instructional texts, historical works, natural history guides, and works on environmental conservation. All books produced by The Mountaineers are aimed at fulfilling the club's mission.

Send or call for our catalog of more than 300 outdoor titles:

The Mountaineers Books
1001 SW Klickitat Way, Suite 201
Seattle, WA 98134
1-800-553-4453 / e-mail: mbooks@mountaineers.org

Other titles you may enjoy from the Mountaineers Books:

MOUNTAINEERING: THE FREEDOM OF THE HILLS, 6ᵀᴴ EDITION
Edited by Graydon and Hanson
Completely revised and expanded edition of the classic text on climbing and mountaineering techniques—required reading for all climbers.

MOUNT MCKINLEY: ICY CROWN OF NORTH AMERICA, Beckey
Portrait of a great climbing challenge, from its natural history to influence on natives, prospectors, and those who have been drawn to its summit. With personal accounts by the author.

MOUNT MCKINLEY: THE PIONEER CLIMBS, Moore
Highlights of climbs on McKinley from initial explorations up to the 1940s; maps, historical photos.

ALASKA'S PARKLANDS: THE COMPLETE GUIDE, Simmerman
Guide to national and state parks and wild areas—location, terrain, scenery, wildlife, camping, weather, facilities, access.

55 WAYS TO THE WILDERNESS IN SOUTHCENTRAL ALASKA, 4ᵀᴴ EDITION, Nienhueser & Wolfe
Updated and revised classic guide to year-round hiking, skiing, and snowshoeing.

DISCOVER SOUTHEAST ALASKA WITH PACK AND PADDLE, 2ᴺᴰ EDITION, Piggott
Fifty-eight hikes in areas from Ketchikan to Skagway, plus a 12-day paddle trip from Juneau to Angoon.

ANIMAL TRACKS: ALASKA, Stall
Tracks and information on more than 40 animals common to the state. Book or poster, sold separately.

MAC'S FIELD GUIDES: ALASKAN WILDLIFE, MacGowan & Sauskojus
Two-sided plastic laminated card developed by a teacher of marine science. Color drawings, common and scientific names, information on size and habitat.

Outdoor Books by the Experts

Whatever the season, whatever your sport, The Mountaineers Books has the resources for you. Our FREE CATALOG includes over 350 titles on climbing, hiking, mountain biking, paddling, backcountry skiing, snowshoeing, adventure travel, natural history, mountaineering history, and conservation, plus dozens of how-to books to sharpen your outdoor skills.

All of our titles can be found at or ordered through your local bookstore or outdoor store. Just mail in this card or call us at 800·553·4453 for your free catalog. Or send us an e-mail at mbooks@mountaineers.org.

Name _____

Address _____

City _____ State _____ Zip+4 _____ - _____

E-mail _____

516-6

Outdoor Books by the Experts

Whatever the season, whatever your sport, The Mountaineers Books has the resources for you. Our FREE CATALOG includes over 350 titles on climbing, hiking, mountain biking, paddling, backcountry skiing, snowshoeing, adventure travel, natural history, mountaineering history, and conservation, plus dozens of how-to books to sharpen your outdoor skills.

All of our titles can be found at or ordered through your local bookstore or outdoor store. Just mail in this card or call us at 800·553·4453 for your free catalog. Or send us an e-mail at mbooks@mountaineers.org.

Please send a catalog to my friend at:

Name _____

Address _____

City _____ State _____ Zip+4 _____ - _____

E-mail _____

516-6

BUSINESS REPLY MAIL
FIRST-CLASS MAIL   PERMIT NO. 85063   SEATTLE, WA

POSTAGE WILL BE PAID BY ADDRESSEE

THE MOUNTAINEERS BOOKS
1001 SW KLICKITAT WAY STE 201
SEATTLE WA 98134-9975

BUSINESS REPLY MAIL
FIRST-CLASS MAIL   PERMIT NO. 85063   SEATTLE, WA

POSTAGE WILL BE PAID BY ADDRESSEE

THE MOUNTAINEERS BOOKS
1001 SW KLICKITAT WAY STE 201
SEATTLE WA 98134-9975